Kicks, Spits, and Headers
The Autobiographical Reflections of an Accidental Footballer

Paolo Sollier

<.:.Min0r.:.>
.c0mp0siti0ns.

Kicks, Spits, and Headers
The Autobiographical Reflections of an Accidental Footballer
Paolo Sollier

Preface by Sandro Mezzadra
Translated by Steven Colatrella
Edited by Stevphen Shukaitis

ISBN 978-1-57027-393-3

Cover & interior design by Acid FC (www.acidfc.com)

Released by Minor Compositions 2022
Colchester / New York / Port Watson

Minor Compositions is a series of interventions & provocations drawing from autonomous politics, avant-garde aesthetics, and the revolutions of everyday life.

Minor Compositions is an imprint of Autonomedia
www.minorcompositions.info
minorcompositions@gmail.com

Distributed by Autonomedia
PO Box 568 Williamsburgh Station
Brooklyn, NY 11211

www.autonomedia.org
info@autonomedia.org

PREFACE

1.

I was a kid in 1975. That Sunday was not different from many others. With my father and my younger brother, we were heading East, on the highway from Savona to Genoa. The so-called "Morandi bridge," which would catastrophically collapse 43 years later, always produced a kind of sense of vertigo in me. It gave the impression that it directly led to our beloved destination, i.e., the stadium of Genoa. On that day, October 5, our club, Sampdoria, played against Lazio. But this is not the reason why I remember that day very well. On September 27, five Spanish comrades, members of the revolutionary organizations ETA and FRAP, had been executed by the Fascist regime. They would turn out to be the last executions in Spain, two months before Francisco Franco's death. A minute of silence had been proclaimed in all Italian stadiums at the beginning of the games. But there was no silence in Genoa (as well as, I guess, elsewhere in Italy). The *whole* "gradinata sud" (the popular sector of the stadium where Sampdoria fans use to gather) stood up, with clenched fists, shouting *Spagna libera, Spagna rossa* ("Free Spain, Red Spain"). I still remember the deep emotion, the sense of sharing something bigger than football that I felt in that moment. And I use to think of that experience as an important threshold in a process of politicization that was already underway due to family stories of resistance against Nazi-fascism but also to the rebellious environment surrounding me while I was growing up.

It is just a personal anecdote, of course. But speaking with many friends (male friends, I must underscore it) I have often heard similar stories. More generally, the stadium has been in the 1970s for many people a training place in Italy, not merely in the sense that they became familiar with techniques to confront the police, but also because they had a chance to experiment with practices of community building among friends that in a way resonated with the ones promoted by the revolutionary movement in the wider society. And the transition to political militancy was in many cases smooth. Organized fans groups took up denominations that were clear references to revolutionary organizations – from the *Brigate Rossonere* (A.C. Milan) to the *Collettivo Autonomo Viola* (Fiorentina) and to *Fedayn* (A.S. Roma) to name a few. Workers' and proletarian behaviors that were prompting the radicalization of class struggle in the country found powerful echoes in the chants, in the attitudes, and in the modes of being together of young fans in the stadiums. This is not to say that all organized fans clubs in the 1970s were leftist. The opposite is true, and readers will for instance encounter in Paolo Sollier's book "the fans of Lazio," or, to be more precise, "the Lazio fascists." While Lazio organized fans have a long history of far-right politics (that continues today), in the 1970s there were several other fascist fans groups, and particularly in cities like Milan and Rome that have two major football clubs local "derbies" were characterized by clashes that had a clear political imprinting. Stadiums were therefore the stage for the representation and enactment of the tensions and violent conflicts that tore apart Italian society.

2.

Readers should bear in mind this picture of Italian stadiums in the 1970s while approaching *Kicks, Spits, and Headers*. Paolo Sollier was definitely not the only leftist footballer in that decade. But he gained an iconic status for a number of reasons. He was really an "accidental footballer," with a biographic background that he shared with many youngsters around 1968. In that year he enrolled at the University of Turin to study political sciences, but he soon quit to work in the FIAT factories that were the epicenter of the "Hot Autumn" of 1969 (anticipated in Turin by the great workers' uprising of Corso Traiano in July). Sollier's life in those years, as he tells in the first pages of the book, was entirely immersed in the dynamics of the movement. Sharing living spaces, mixing up relationships and revolutionary politics, moving from one group to another were experiences common to an entire generation. Even when he became a professional footballer, his style, his beard were clear traces of an existential and political difference, made famous by a photo in which he greets fans with clenched fist. Sollier was not only attacked by fascist fans like the ones of Lazio, he was also criticized by the establishment for politicizing football. And he conversely became an icon for the left, even beyond the militants of *Avanguardia Operaia* – the Marxist-Leninist organization to which Sollier belonged at the time of writing the book.

It is also important to note that Sollier played for two years in Perugia, a kind of outsider club that in the second half of the 1970s challenged the established powers of Italian football, deploying under trainer Ilario Castagner a specific variant of "total football" (in 1978/1979 Perugia ranked second behind A.C. Milan). Sollier's militant gaze on the "system" of Italian football is therefore a gaze from the margin (from the "province") and one can say that his attempt, documented in the book, was to bring the rupture of '68 within and against the world of football. His remarks on "rooting as a social illness," on the politics and political economy of sports, on the Footballers Association are all fragments of a wider discourse to be collectively constructed and enacted within the framework of the radical transformation of society that was underway in Italy as well as elsewhere in those years. While this is definitely an interesting aspect of *Kicks, Spits, and Headers*, readers will probably find even more engaging today the narrative of Sollier's attempt to balance political militancy, professional football at the highest level, and the existential challenges confronted by a man in his late 20s. Sex (and love) are everywhere in the book. "Pussy," Sollier writes, "is one of the favorite subjects of conversation" among footballers, "along with pussy, and also pussy." "In the end," he further comments, "there is no way out of it, everything is sex." Flirts and liaisons (even with a fascist girl) fill the pages of the book, between a game and a demonstration. By today's standards Sollier's words may often sound as bordering on some form of sexism. And nevertheless, he claims speaking of one of his relations: "Now I feel 'feminist' because I feel that it concerns me." And feminism is also quite present in the book, for instance when Sollier replies to a rightist journalist who criticizes him for raising the fist through a parallel between that gesture and the "feminist symbol of hands forming a pussy stand for recognition, joy, peace among themselves, but war on sexism." Take it as a tale of the multiple and contested ways in which the feminist revolution in Italy challenged sexism even among comrades and within the movement.

3.

There is no need to stress that the world of football critically described by Sollier is largely history. Stadiums themselves were transformed in the following decades, and the logic of business (sometimes connected to organized crime) reshaped even the structure and action of organized fans groups. The free spaces of sociability and encounter that had characterized the social formation of the stadium in the experience of previous generations of young fans have been drastically standardized and eventually subsumed under a capitalist logic. Moreover, since the early 1990s the far right took over, often in a violent way, many *curve* – the curved parts of the stands in Italian stadiums, seated behind the goals and home to the most intense fans. While in the 1970s social movements and class struggle had a clear politicizing effect on fans, stadium chants began already in the following decade to be adapted to political demonstrations, signaling a kind of reversal in the working and manifestations of hegemony. As far as footballers are concerned, they have remained in Italy largely untouched by the wave of at least symbolic politicization that has been manifest in other European countries particularly in the wake of Black Lives Matter. The recent European Championship was a clear sign of that, with the Italian team confused and undecided in front of other footballers who took a knee at the beginning of games. In the age of Colin Kaepernick, LeBron James, or Romelu Lukaku, Italian football remains a kind of self-referential bubble, while in other sports there is no shortage of (mainly female) persons who openly take a stand against racism and sexism.

And nevertheless, football continues to remain in Italy a passion that involves many young (and less young) activists. Although in completely different conditions with respect to the 1970s people meet around football and ask questions that lead them to engage in social centers and in other social and political projects. Leftist organized fans groups exist in many cities, and they are often engaged in European anti-fascist networks. An event like the *Mondiali Antirazzisti* ("Anti-racist World Cup"), that exists since 1996, brings together each year dozens of teams and hundreds of fans from several European countries for a festival of "sport and struggle." And the anti-racist characterization of the event is particularly important if one considers that stadiums have been relevant sites for the spread of racism over the last decades in Italy as well as elsewhere. All these initiatives, and many others, clearly aim at making football a field of struggle while at the same time cultivating the passion for football. One can say that, in a different historical conjuncture, Paolo Sollier's aim was quite similar. Reading *Kicks, Spits, and Headers* today allows readers to explore from a specific viewpoint the landscape of politics and football in the turbulent 1970s in Italy. It also delivers us the fragmentary contours of a project that deserves to be translated onto the conditions of our present.

Sandro Mezzadra

KICKS, SPITS, AND HEADERS
The Autobiographical Reflections
of an Accidental Footballer

I look at myself and laugh. I see myself stuck in a comic strip like Snoopy, a bundle of clothes on a pole over my shoulder, with a word balloon reading: "here's the famous footballer leaving Turin…"

Famous my ass. Who knows what I'm getting myself into. Three years ago I had refused to live this kind of life. I was supposed to go from the Cossatese, the Football team based in the city of Cossato, to Lecco; there was a manager there, Longoni, who had fallen in love with me. But I also had to leave home, and begin that utterly ill-fated commune. It had been more important to stay in Turin, and make a decisive cut in the emotional economic umbilical cord connecting me to my parents; push myself to finally into being autonomous, with my own floor to clean, bills to pay, my own toilet to fix; to have a home, a kennel, a den to stay in, to get angry in, to get laid in.

Now, instead, there was nothing to hold me there. No girl, all of them having fallen off my emotional Richter scale; earthquakes having razed them all to the ground. No political commitment biting my lone wolf tail. Certainly not the commune, or maybe I should say the madhouse, or the four monkeys that had recently been living together. The last stage of this communitarian sack race had started a year earlier: Gigi and I had survived the preceding storms, Andrea and Tito had arrived by accident. Andrea from a demonstration for Chile.

Arm the MIR, "Hey do you have a place to live?" *Christian Democrats: Murderers.* "Yeah, it's pretty empty." *Frei is a killer.*

"I'll come and stay for a few months." *Comrade Allende will be vindicated.* "Come and stay." *Never again without a rifle.*

And he had come there to be number three, to play left back, the Facchetti of the situation. He would have played some defense, and then infiltrated the first open corridor. Naturally, along with a corridor, there would have to be rooms, a kitchen, a bathroom; a whole house in other words. But the right pass never arrived, and so he moved in with us.

After a month, Tito; he was dragged in from the town of Torre Pellice, near Turin. He showed up one evening and starting talking, standing in the doorway, "So here's my situation…I have a wife, and I have a girlfriend who also has a son. I haven't lived with my wife for a year, and I haven't been working for more than a year. I'm a mess. But I've decided to rebuild my life…." He put down the bag with that wolfish smile, and he started washing the dishes.

Living together, becoming friends, is like compressing an explosive mixture. The better you get along, the more you compress things. The more you compress things, the more explosive they become. At the first spark they explode. Everyone gets thrown clear, distant, like a splinter or a piece of a star. Compression, friendship, then you start up again with other people. Then come new explosions, other human projectiles, and new bombs to trigger.

And so it was with us. And now we are all blown apart. The Gigi fragment to grab onto the braids of his Danish dream; Tito, hunting for work, and looking out for vipers; Andrea in the continuing struggle of writing his book bit by bit on a recording machine. He interviews them all: workers, the unemployed, leaders, the broken down, the burned out, the drugged out. Naturally he will never finish it.

Finally me, the fragment that broke off and went on to play football. Finally I will know that despite all my different fears, I'm happy: no more being the compromised footballer, neither footballer nor student, neither activist nor lone wolf, no more Serie C, caught between the intellectual mosquitoes of Vercelli and the train to Turin. I will know if I am worth something in football, and I will know also – the first fear – if I'll sell my out my ass to fit in.

Aside from playing football, travel, practicing, will this professional football swallow up my mind? Or will I be able to live my life without having to follow a path that is laid out for me, to be able to live the way I want to?

These are my thoughts as the FIAT 500 rowed its way (so to speak) toward Perugia, ten hours of highway, memories, and questions. All my roots in Turin have been cut, who knows for how long, those in Perugia who await me, who knows how they'll welcome me? Who will I find there? Will my teammates be nice and boring, and will the manager Castagner rhyme well enough with Sollier?

Green Umbria, Red Umbria, Jazz Umbria is all that I know. We can add a little bit of Saint Francis, Jacapone da Todi, and the wolves of Gubbio. I feel like I am going to live in my own ignorance.

I arrive there. Perugia, glued to the horizon, my home, looked for and found in a single day. I am really a highly-privileged emigrant.

I think of the real emigrants, snatched from their lands, thrown into octopus cities, seen with suspicion, cut off from society, sleeping in basements, under staircases, at the train stations. I saw them with my own eyes, and it makes these slivers of fear I have seem ridiculous. It is that old habit of mine of feeling a fingernail on my own back more than I feel a pickaxe in someone else's.

Preseason training camp: every footballer's nightmare – twenty days to get strength, elasticity, the desire to run, back into your muscles. That first week where every hour of lost sleep, every snack between meals, every fuck that was a little too strenuous, are repaid with sweat and curses. On the other hand, it is the only retreat that everyone goes through almost willingly; you get tired, but you rest, you bust your ass, but your physique gets put back into shape. It's an adjustment of all the screws that were stripped bare by a month of holiday. And it also lasts you all year. It is a useful medicine, drunk down with a grimace, but it works. How many grimaces then depends on where you are coming from, what kind of relationship you manage to have with the people there, if you are able to get outside of the circle of the team; otherwise by dint of seeing the same faces you start to go crazy, and soon the knives start flying.

For us there's Norcia, the Christian-Democrat town of Saint Benedict, but also of Brancaleone. And "The Incredible Army of Brancaleone" seems to be this Perugia team, nearly all new, a lot of us from Serie C, not sent back there for another year by a hair. We look ourselves in the face and seem to ask ourselves, "but just where do we want to go?"

I would like to go to that blonde, but ultimately, I am always a little clumsy. And in any case, she doesn't give a shit about me; I have to open a new battle front.

One of the ways footballers get to know each other is in the shower. Seeing each other's little guitars. Who has a big one and who has a little one, who has one that is a little crooked, who's been circumcised. There's the total disconnect between the overall physique and the dick. The slightly overweight guy who's got one that's long and thin, the gangly guy who has a short thick one; the little guy who has a cowbell hanging between his legs, and the superman who has a tiny one.

Pussy is one of the favorite subjects of conversation, along with pussy, and also pussy. All the jokes are about Zumbo (the nickname given to my friend Giancarlo Raffaeli), who has an abominably big one, and so who knows what heavenly experiences he distributes around town; or Sergio, with the dome and big umbrella that provides everyone with shade. Naturally the sexual theories according to which the size of the penis is of minor importance are dismissed. Love is sold in grams, fucking is measured in meters. It's a part of the role of the famous man against whom women break themselves to pieces, like moths inside a light bulb. And if the moths are around, anxious to have you touch them, and insert the golden calf in them, then it makes sense that this viewpoint persists. It's idiotic, but it persists. It persists even if those engaging in it are married people, with kids. I wonder, in these families, with these wives, what kind of relationship is there? These dickhead comments about women being holes, do these guys say those things at home? Or are they two-faced, the perfect husband at home, then fucking for thrills when they're out?

Moreover, the wives of footballers are always a mysterious object (subject, sorry): they live in a reflected light, they follow along when he is sold to another city, they watch his kids, they wait for him to return home from battle. It is a kind of old-fashioned way of doing things, one that's collapsing all over the world. How long will it take in our case?

Castagner pretty much leaves us alone, so some are able to steal a hurried fuck, but more often, it's platonic sitting together on the stairs of the monument to Saint Benedict, with his three fingers in heaven's ass, we with three stairs up ours. We talk, we tell stories, we laugh. This team is nice, we feel fine. Marconcini says we're going to have a big season.

I was saying that I like this super-thin, edgy blonde. She's the friend and the sister of two witches. One of them discovered death when she read my hand, a broken line, and then a fortune line that goes up and down, a strong character line, but with a tendency to be self-critical. Strong sensuality, and a tendency to being unfaithful that is so clear, it's even faithful. The other pulled a corpse right out of my eyes: "You had a great love end badly." I would like to know who hasn't. But her instead, the anti-witch, I like a lot. She's of the race of women without busts, where you seem to look at an empty town square, restful and exciting inside, as if it were fated to be.

She had a fault however, which is written on the wall by those who put manifestos around town: she's kind of fascist. And I told her she turns her nose up at things as if they stink, and she denied it. And we remained there, me without looking for what stunk, not in her nose, but everywhere; she, of a good right wing background, with her own reasons for all those bombs around; but at least she hadn't saved any of them for me.

With Mariella, in the magic of Perugia. We walk *main-dans-la-main* until our shadows disappear below us. They print onto the asphalt before us, and they suffocate me; we don't realize it, but those shadows holding hands are already the end of us. Those two dark lovers seem like rings of a chain that's already broken, marriage rings of torture, fingers in the eye of the storm. When she goes away, she leaves me alone twice. And solitude is my first life in Perugia. So I think and rethink about my life, I walk through the lanes of this wonderful city under the rainfall.

When it rains, I feel like I'm in the mountains; the odor of wet plants reaches the doors of my house. And at the door I feel like those old folks that left for a week to cut the hay; they stayed up in the mountains until they got it all done. It makes me imagine them in the evening, sitting on the steps, drinking a coffee looking into the dark, just as I was doing. Except that I didn't come to cut the hay, and I am in a city. Christ, one that is full of people that I don't know. I begin to understand how so many young athletes started to talk such bullshit, to get all messed up. They come and get you, and they take you away from your home, they stick you somewhere in some fucking beautiful city. Then it's all your own shit. You have to perform when you're on the football field; the rest is up to you.

If this happens to you when you are already grown and developed, no problem. But if you arrive at this at age sixteen, it's a real mess. A lot of them become fauna of various bars, always far away from whatever is happening, dazed by the idea of having a career, of becoming one of the trading cards. Because this is the philosophy around football: make your own way, your own money, your own success, your own house, your own woman. The most fucked-up individualism, with two even worse outcomes: either you succeed, and you become one of the privileged, a rich man who defends his power, in fact a reactionary, like all those that have a privilege to defend. Or else you fold, and you go bang your head, with the same approach, against something else. In fact footballers committed to something else besides football are rare. I don't mean big things, but just being interested in what is happening in the world, in knowing something, in being informed and critical; at least not taking in the television like it was God. It is even rare to find a tendency to socialize, and this stands in contradiction to the very idea of teamwork; on the field it is all for one and one for all; off the field everyone puts his ideological clothes back on and has relationships with the others that may even be genial, but which are disconnected and superficial. So it happens that you play for the same team for years, ass to ass with each other, and then you leave as though you had never met, while looking to find friends in other settings. This is the obvious consequence of a mere work relationship between people from very different cultures and places; for whom if it were not for football, they would never have a reason to say or do anything together. Certainly this mass lack of commitment makes me feel rather alone, even if it makes me laugh to see how it is presented in the newspapers: the red footballer, or the intellectual one, or maybe the footballer political militant. It would be worth explaining to them that politically I am in the middle of a shit storm. For more than a year I have been a lone wolf, crying in the wilderness, trying to make pigs fly. And realizing that it can't go on like this is certainly no solution. I stick to my useless barking and watch, impotent, stoned, and comfortable.

LONE WOLF
There, it's done
I don't burst into flames anymore
the revolutionary
matches
or the constipated
tricolor flame
at most just leave me
singed.
The Chilean scalding
and the incandescent stones
travel inside me
at the speed
of light cooling off.
By now they're plastic
so they don't burn, they just poison.

But for them I'm just the different footballer, it's comfortable.

"They" are the sports press in general, plus the political press, which when they report on sports do more damage than a storm does. Of course it isn't right to tie all the herbs into one bundle: *Il Messaggero* or *Paese Sera* are not *La Nazione* fortunately, and *Tuttosport* is not *Stadio*. But this idiotic idea of someone being a celebrity gets around, and if someone is a celebrity you have to write about them. It doesn't matter if you are getting to the bottom of something or writing crap, what's important is to get the headline, to take the photo, to make the news. That old, idiotic sensationalism, nothing more; but it bothers you all the same.

I don't get along with people as a footballer. It is inevitable that this start is going to be uphill. I'm down on the canvas, politically lost and disintegrated, ridiculous when I play, my "loves" dispersed around the world, far away. Now I understand also why the average footballer is married or super-engaged: if you marry, you bring everything with you, roots, furniture, chamber-pot. You always have your world that works for you, your den, with sex and affection guaranteed.

Friends come. Also, other people come, thanks to the power of fame which I did not know about in Turin. Like Enzo, making the rounds of some nearby communities. It's clear that if I am in Africa and run across an Italian, he is saliva of my saliva. So is a Torinese in Perugia; I was never friends with him up there, if anything ferocious ideological opponents. So how can we be friends here? I look at him and it's as if I see things from home: Borgo Vanchiglia, San Giulio, the River Po. Like he's just a postcard. In any case, even real friends aren't anything to shout about: they come, but then they go. And who fills the hole they leave? Here I know a lot of people, but no one to truly get wrapped up with. Girls are a total disaster. To feed my starved little "bird" there is nothing for it but the poorest birdseed, five against one, the jerk. Why not? What, I should go to whores? Or repress it till it comes out my eyes? And in any case it's not so bad, let them say what they want, all those experts, sexologists, and moralists.

Martine is among the phone calls of desire. Martine is the latest Mohammad to come down from the mountain; so my reverse doping can continue. Transfusions, blood compressed inside, strength. Then they take it away from you and the weakness returns, the tiredness, the deck chair. That then is your natural state having passed through the gas chamber of having company. Castagner says that this Frenchwoman has ruined me; just the idea of fucking seems to debone you. Ridiculous. It's just that September is black for me too. I am a one-man refugee camp. I can barely stand on my own two feet, as if the blood didn't know what direction it is supposed to flow in. This is the exhaustion of preseason training camp, your muscles rendered senile by training. Then it passes, and you return to form, but in the meantime, it's all Martine's fault.

With her returns my imbecilic emotional strategy, or being unable to stay together. All it takes is a week for me to feel suffocated, stuck in an amorous jar, insufferable, dying to escape. She says she understands, but at the same time her eyes trace out a thick, sweet net that entraps me. She tells me a dream: I was walking on a map.

You saw me walk
on top of a map
between the crazy borders
of your dream.
But you
are the map, walked on
consumed
and now folded up
and put away
in a drawer.

I wanted her to leave. Then, closed in the fist, closed in the train, she and all my bollocks, echoing the sorrow of being alone. And there's nothing at home that responds, that echoes in reply, that has caught and held her gestures; you just turn around and you see the emptiness, the solitude, the dizziness, that softly take over your muscles. Like hanging onto a mountain cliff, in the fog, warning of the danger, the effort it will take, the determination; I talk to myself, I warn myself, I reassure myself; I know the way after all. Then the fog lifts, and I find myself on another cliff, eternal, that never ends, never begins, that isn't even there. It's a moment, an exhalation, a getting better, a feeling myself in different bodies, and in different minds. Then the shadow passes again over my eyes, and goes on to close the hole up again. And we are back to normal, putting your nuts to the grindstone. A little while later another dizziness, dizzinesses and chasms that open onto each other, recompose, and imprint themselves on the memory, like fossils.

You half-smile, she half-smiles too, so together you have a whole one. And it stays in that piazza forever, like those halves of coins, or medals, held together by distance and the instant they are put back together it is time to throw them out. In Parma.

In Parma, on the field. With my adversary, we both walk away from the ball. A kick comes my way. Hey no, I ask him, why do you have to give me a kick like that, while I am standing still? He looks at me a while, "Yeah" he says, "you're right really." Funny and splendid. His name's Andreoli.

In Parma, after having read the incredible Gabriel Garcia Marquez, and his great *Incredible and Sad Tale of Innocent Erèndira*, I go buy for three thousand lire *Fogli di Diario* by Carlo Cassola. But I swear it's the last time. I read just enough of him to be contented, and from that just enough comes the squalid impression of emptiness, of superficiality, of air that's been fried. And at least he was honest. No, smuggling in these things so as to create internal conflict, or digging deep, or existential drilling. It's like petroleum: make a hole there and you know it will come up, always the same and always profitable.

But you need to burn it too.

About this signor *Frate Mitra*. I say the Red Brigades aren't needed for the class struggle. They are political cartoons, too distant from the struggles of the masses; comrades who have lost their way and become dangerous.

But this Friar spits in your face. To think I admired him too. I met him years ago, while still entangled with the dissenting Catholics, when I thought that the problems of the Third World could be solved by collecting paper and rags, to get the money to buy them spades and hoes. Then came the first '69 of my life, everything turned upside down, the experiences in the factory, the July 3rd of Corso Traiano, the batons that rained down on us, me escaping up a tree. And the people of the Third World taught me that machine guns plow better than shovels. But at the time that brother, who had passed through the Foreign Legion, was a great example of "nonviolence," of "love" of "paying in person." Now I find him to be a spy, and not only here. In Bolivia, on his way to buy bread, he sold out a guerilla leader; and in Chile, he stayed at the Italian Embassy, to do some dirty stuff.

FRIAR BRAGGART
Didn't you say
to not use violence
brother machinegun?
And once you used it
didn't you speak of
revolutionary violence?
And didn't you
have a son
with a Bolivian woman?
And didn't you tell
Of the open veins
Of South America?
And wasn't it
all sold

*already
long before
you sold yourself
Brother spy?*

Certainly, between spies and generals, coups d'état and secret services, it's a big mess. It's all coming out as if from the asshole of a mule: bit by bit the asshole enlarges, it dilates and opens up and this fascist shit comes out, ever bigger, smelly, full of branches of thorny roses. Out come the generals, the financiers, the consultants, the cleanup men, all in this big, complicated shit. I can already see how it ends: expelled, kicked out in this useless shit, burned out, shit out by those that have been discovered and no longer useful, the hole closes back up, pink as ever, and nothing changes. The mule is this State, even if it would be more correct to call it a donkey. And its asshole is well-protected.

I's certainly already better than when Pietro Valpreda was made into a monster in the pages of *Corriere della Sera*. Thanks to the power of mobilization, of kicks to the donkey, something came out; but who knows what else still has to come out. The danger is the habit of covering things up; people get angry and then they forget, they get angry and then they forget, until they forget to get angry; they get used to these generals in South America. On this the comrades have to put their foot down hard, even at the cost of getting calluses.

Jokes about me. Perugia vs. Foggia: why is Sollier still running so hard, there's hardly any time left, and they are winning three to one. He has to, he's in Lotta Continua.

Or: in Brescia, Sollier has to score, because the goalkeeper for the other team is named Borghese.

And another: there's a cop that's going around saying he saw me early that morning in Corso Vannucci with a chicken over my shoulder and ten cats on leashes. They actually asked me if it was true: I should do it for real.

Who does it for real is the team. Nobody joked around even a little, not even us. We are in first place, we are playing well, we make the other teams look foolish. Every now and then we look ourselves in the eyes and take the piss out of the monument in Norcia. Where do we want to end up? Nowhere in particular, but we are getting there all the same. Glory to Castagner.

Yeah, Ilario. A somewhat shy guy with like four ideas rolling around in his head, none of them very complicated, and with strong convictions. As a trainer, he is alright. As a man, he is a disaster. He knows how to work muscles, but not how to work the minds of his players; especially the ones that don't play. He should talk to them, keep their morale up, get them involved. Instead, nothing. You have to read the newspapers if you want to know the formation, if you are playing, if you're on the bench, in penalties, or being fucked up the ass. This really, really sucks.

His good luck is to have built a team taking into account the football characteristics of the players and to have found that they also were united as personalities. People who get along together, who laugh, joke, help each other out; who don't need psychological support from the manager that isn't there to give it.

The Swiss may be really clean outside, but are really dirty inside; at least that nearly half of them that want to kick out all the immigrant workers. William Tell, instead of the apple, should have split his kid's head, and those of all the rest of his descendants; these cheese-making bar bouncers, bank buddies of Michele Sindona, with their crappy watches. Assholes, exploiters, and canton-dwellers.

At the start of my lone-wolfization, a year and more ago, I gave half a thought to the PCI, but it was probably just the search for a refuge, the simplest and easiest thing to do. It gave me the feeling of getting inside of an armored tank (without implying anything), and by comparison the extra-leftists were like bicycles pulling a little wagon. In the PCI, everything is certain, you have the line and the counter-line, your back and your ass covered, all ready, everything organized. But your eyes are covered too. In short, the PCI gets worse all the time, and responds less and less to the desire and the need for struggle; it continues to draw strength from the historical tradition, and hats off to that, but with this strong antifascist fabric, day by day sewn to death and shot full of holes, with this fabric how do they expect to cover up all the shit of today? The good old Party has become sedate, domesticated; it does everything according to the (bourgeois) rules, it respects the neighbors; and deep down it makes compromises and it hits the brakes.

It gets bigger, certainly it gets bigger, it opens the door to everyone. I have never seen so many Communist bosses as there are today, and please excuse the contradiction. But the calculation is simple: if you are on the left, maybe even on the Red city council, you get a much more peaceful factory floor. What? you want the workers to struggle against the entrepreneurial comrade? That'll never happen, don't worry, the union will see to that.

That's why I renew my membership in Avanguardia Operaia. There I will find friends too. After all, if I don't find any among the comrades, where will I find them?

An opportunistic move, someone might say. Sure. But among the many tasks of a political organization there is also providing a home to its members. Nothing more, nothing less.

I already talked to the comrades: I am going back to the University. The very vaunted and backward University of Perugia: it's a combination of modern and ancient, of novelty and frustration, of vitality and rust. A Red governing body. Lots of comrades. A good place, I told myself. And it's here that I really find the traditions that command, imprison, and suffocate you. The life of the comrades follows in the footsteps of their fathers: grow up, look for a job, get married, produce a kid. There are a few holes in the sweater, like towns or couples finally destroyed, where no one sticks their nose in. There nothing you can do: these same comrades combine great political maturity with great personal imbecility, indecision and stupidity.

I have to pose the problem.

The fantastic part, and together with it the stupid part of some things is that they don't have other boundaries for themself and for themselves. There are satisfactions in life that you can't communicate to anyone else. Who enjoys thinking about my very fattened up first love getting married to a very thin guy? And with whom can I share my rage for a dead friend being insulted by being defined "a good soul"? Who can understand catching flies and letting them get sucked dry by spiders and then pissing on the web? To whom can I inject the joy, the sensation, the place of my first jerk off, my dick all blood-engorged and red? Who celebrates with me the downfall of that kid that they always presented to me as a model for my entire childhood?

I have to do it alone, subtly, implacably; the incommunicability, the solitude, the intellectual desert (camels and camels, just don't think about it), all really amount to this; crumbs, specks, fallen hairs, boils, stupid lice imprisoned in the consciousness. No one can understand, no one can put them back; and at least if they'd stay calm, but they absolutely don't. Under a big ass pile of ashes they are always lit. Yeah, eternal flame.

Like looking up at the stars from a pile of poison ivy. Nothing to do but scratch.

Let in criticism at all costs, bring it into everything. Have fun at the movies, but be able to see what's going on inside it, what's behind it, and how it works. Don't let yourself be conditioned by contrarianism (so that your critique becomes knives pointed at all costs, without being "freely" open to emotional responses), but rather disengage somewhat neutrally from the cinema, confining it to the two or three hours spent there, or see it as not having to have other ideas for that time. Being spectators and critics, maybe not simultaneously, is how criticism can easily get the spectator in its sights as well.

My first bad act on the field. Perugia vs. Avellino, we win, there's very little time left, free kick in the penalty area for them, me inside the wall. Carlo Ripari gets in front of me, and he starts to elbow me and to give me a hip check: I majestically stuck my foot right up his butt crack. Naturally the referee didn't see it. Afterwards, I felt really satisfied, an outlaw and a smart one at that. Those that are looking for it, I told myself, you gotta give it to them. Later I felt ashamed. It's the first time that a foot wins Independence and at the same time gets me into trouble.

Pulled away from putting up posters on my wall at home, I returned to putting up manifestos on the walls of the University. I have a method to doing it that is the envy of all. Sure, after having upholstered up every hole in the Palazzo Nuovo in Turin for two years, this here is all too easy. The walls are covered in no time.

The poison ivy no.

I found another girl…But who remembers Jonzac the same way I do?

That moist moon, those sundowns that glowed on Hanne's skin. And when I returned there two years later, my anxieties rummaging through the grass, ever more grass and less scrap metal, there was no sign of our time together. Her meter-long braids, her big toe sliced clean off by a washing machine, the chickens that pecked me while I lay inside the sleeping bag…

No one remembers this, nobody would give a fig to talk about it. Just me down there to die between her arms, to feel her undressing my fantasy. And that's all. Shit.

Twelve December, the birthday boy, Perugia, the extra-leftist in the Hall of Notaries. And a comrade of Avanguardia Operaia comes up to ask me for an autograph. I blasted him.

If with others I explain myself, and that's the right thing to do, with this guy I didn't even try to show patience. I told him to go fuck himself. "You're right, but look…." I told him that being revolutionaries means being different, means changing things, from the big things to the little crap like this. Indeed, this is how to solve things, change things, throw out the stupid crap, have the courage of your convictions. It doesn't make sense anymore being a comrade in the piazza or in the factory or at school if that choice doesn't have repercussions that boomerang like a whip on your habits, if it doesn't take them by surprise and throw them overboard. Otherwise you find yourself with a crust of struggle, but inside you are soft and mushy, incapable, like a clam version of yourself.

This issue of signing autographs is really a dangerous mania, precisely because it is considered a stupid little thing. It is one of the first steps toward accepting things as they are. The world is made up of important people and unimportant people. The important ones are to be idolized, and placed a step above the others. And it is the duty of the unimportant ones to chase down the important ones and to return with a souvenir, whether it is a signature, or a strand of hair or a fuck, in any case the easier it is to show off, the better it is. "See, Rivera signed an autograph for me, I'm lucky."

These hurried scribbles are an example of one of the rules of this system: to give value to things that don't have any. And to do so means having to create a whole series of false desires for false needs. This one happens to be the stupidest, but it is not really different than the need for a better-looking automobile, or more elegant clothes. It is an ideology that they bombard you with from the time you are born to the day you die, in order to hopefully make you desire a first-class funeral.

Of course when a child asks you for an autograph and you refuse he gives you a dirty look. He feels robbed of something precious, they have taught him that it is worth who knows what. Not signing them has gotten me criticized and cursed out endless times. They say he is someone that doesn't give a damn about the fans, he looks down at them, he puts on airs.

But it's the opposite, because it is much easier to sign something than to stop and explain or discuss. Because it is a trifling, which doesn't cost anything and yet is taken to be a victory, or a sign of belonging. Because it is actually always a way to avoid the fan, to get rid of an irritation, instead of making someone happy. And it makes you into a saint.

I've talked about this in front of classes of children and groups of fans. But why this stupid thing I asked them. Wouldn't it be better if we hung out together a little, if we talked a little about football, if we realized we could have a person-to-person relationship, instead of an imbecile-to-imbecile one? In the end a lot of them said this was okay, that I was right. Like with kids. Why are you asking for an autograph? "Um… because everyone does it." Why don't you ask your friend for an autograph too, or why don't you give me yours? "Because you're famous, and my friends and I aren't."

This song's chorus is really rich: famous equals important equals let me touch you. And then the adults come to the defense of the children: "But at least for the children…" No for god's sake, educate them from the start. And if they are subjected, without the excuse of being little, to all the conditioning, the repression and the mirrors for infants from television to family, it's right that there be some counter-force to restore a rickety balance. It can only do them some good.

Not to mention the fathers that ask you for autographs using their kids as an alibi. They're like the dads that buy a train set for their kid so that they can play with it themselves.

Guido; he was ten years old. Who knows if he has already been reincarnated, if he stole God's plums, if he is still anything at all. I saw him in front of me one evening, while I was in bed, between the dark of the room and the dark of falling asleep. I started to remember with insane precision our last summer together. As if a glacier in my memory had imprisoned those months, had conserved them, and then sent them, unconsciously, to me, and now they had remained unchanged to me. Sure I felt the same physical pain, the same nerves from back then that punched me in the gut, that made me ask myself how it happened. Making me look into that water pad seeking answers, some flight of logic. Making me ask myself if in some pebble, in some piece of tree bark, in some rock, hadn't there remained some memory, some reason why, maybe a photograph. The same complicity for our adventures, mine and his, exhausted but ready to start again, to get our energy back all the way to the end.

Then him on the couch with nothing on to keep the flies off. Without his cursing – God f…without his t-shirt. With his dick incapable of making those four meter pisses. Me at home doubled over with my latest sobs; and those of Paoletta at his funeral.

Then, all at once, the whole story reentered the glacier, and the desire came over me to go look inside the drawer. To still find a trace of him, maybe in the cards. The tarot cards seem to make things happen and to invent them. But instead they go fishing for them. For the future, for yesterday, for the now; they hook something. They inform the breath, the whisper, the footstep. I don't know if I really believe it, but all that unattainable force that whirls around us makes me think of other lives, of a place where we end up, of an eternal wolf pack of the spirit, a peace that you and I can look at, and respond to.

One afternoon in a club in Perugia. It is raining successes, they are coming up out of the ground like mushrooms, and there are those who go immediately to harvest them. I would prefer that the need to do something together, to feel united, to associate together, were something more than meeting up with the plan to yell a lot on Sunday. Fan clubs are an example of a real desire with a bullshit answer to it. The desire to get together, meet each other, talk together, is sacred. But the solution to making that happen remains superficial. Nor does it ask for any serious commitment: you just have to root for Perugia. So if at the club the rich man is shoulder to shoulder with the unimportant poor man, the sport makes them brothers, doesn't it?

No one cares if you feel the need to talk about your problems, how you feel, about what could be done in the city or in your neighborhood, if everything is going well for you, or badly. Let's just get the banners ready and all is well. It's really a shame to see so much creativity, so much energy channeled into the condom of the stadium. Thrown away, wasted. And this doesn't mean that you shouldn't go to the match, not at all. But you need to go more as sportsmen and less as fans. You need to spend the afternoon doing something more useful than leaving the wife at home and going to the bar to talk football.

But we were at the club. Not exactly taxing ourselves to increase the number of fans. Franco D'Attoma, the President, known as "White Pen," makes a nice speech: "The team belongs to everyone, it's yours too, so let them know that you want a new stadium. Today there are four hundred votes here, and there were another two hundred the other day, to give some idea. So those who need to understand will understand that they need to build the stadium."

Endless applause.

Then there's the other big thing: selling shares.

All around there are amazing posters. One is a photo of a guy in ordinary clothes, kicking the ball into the net, and underneath it says, "I too got a piece of Perugia!" People's shareholding they call it. With this story about Perugia belonging to everybody, and this business about "getting a piece" bouncing off every wall, it seems like the sale of (non-voting) shares is a great success. They buy them. That it's a swindle no one doubts. In the shareholder companies that don't exist mainly to make money, like football teams, you will never be paid dividends, and your shares are non-voting, so what are you the owner of except a useless piece of paper, a diploma of stupidity?

No one doubts that it is a rip-off. How can you say "Perugia belongs to everyone," when Perugia belongs to D'Attoma, Ghini, and company, my dear? Wouldn't it be more honest to just open a subscription and say that you will lose this money but will have contributed to lowering the company's deficit? But it works better to misrepresent everything. And what's absurd is that the people fall for it. And here we are in one of the capital cities of the Italian road to communism!

★★★

A phone call from the little fascist blondie. She says I really have to listen to her, at Christmas in Norcia, that she doesn't understand anything anymore…an ideological shift maybe?

In Norcia, I do a "Dutch" retreat, and anyone that doesn't have any is looking for it. In the discotheque, in town, in the rubbish bins.

I have to talk with Grazia, but nothing doing. We talk yeah, but to find something that unites us; we keep our hands away from each other. Then we get cold with each other; then I get pissed off.

Look, usually a retreat is a drag, but you were there, so I was happy to come. And you seem like you don't care at all. And she says, "…but it was the same for me. You're the one going off on your own…." A magnificent fucked up conversation, which in any case knocks down anything knockdownable. Later we dance the danceable, allowing for the fact that I have two left feet (though Mario Scarpa was impressed with all how much I moved), then we go out together.

I won't say it. Everyone knows she's a fascist. And everyone knows I am a comrade. Galliano, the waiter, comes to tell me, right before I leave, that a comrade like me should know better than to do this. And he doesn't say anything else. "I'll write you," he says, and hurries away to serve tables.

What do I need you to tell me, what I already know? And so I come away with the right ventricle beating wildly, but I don't say anything. I let this marvelous corpse live, I keep it far away from my friends, from the choices already made, and from myself.

I can't fall in love. But I also can't not fall in love. It is a splendid synthesis of the opposing extremisms. Far from moving over to our side, she is fascist down to her asshole. She is one of the purists, but that doesn't change anything. Pure shit is still shit. And she has two eyes where I go straight to plant myself. My research on impossible loves has never gone this far afield. I am really absurd.

Speaking of impossible loves, I really thought I was a mental case. Sickly in love in a hopeless situation, out of love immediately whenever it worked out. Then, instead of me being a mental case, I began to think it was destiny, and that led down to loneliness. But, on the contrary, it was just self-defense.

It is essentially the desire to be alone that every once in a while fucks with the desire to be part of a couple. So my brain starts to give birth to antibodies: if things go well with a person I immediately feel like a prisoner, in a cage, lost. If things go badly with someone, here comes the need to run after them, to turn over in bed to feel her presence, to explode. The result: I escape from the ones that want me, the ones I want escape from me. And if they don't escape, I look for them over greater distances.

Bente is the best example. Every time I think of her my brain catches on fire, my eyes get vaporized, my dick falls off, I read my belly button as if hieroglyphics were written on it. But she is in Denmark, well-protected by the distance between us, and by all her other men.

To be sure, this escaping thing is not so simple. Otherwise it would be stupid. One of its root causes is that I do pretty well alone. There's someone that I'd like to be with, and I can't find her. A woman able to stand on her own two feet alone, in a free relationship, where being together also means letting each other be alone, or to be with other people, as it comes, to me, or to her. It's risky. A relationship where you always feel like you're in the crosshairs, with nothing certain, nothing taken for granted, forever defeated. It isn't the usual idea of cheating on someone, and letting them cheat on you. It's a different idea of what a couple is. Or rather, of not being a couple. Of two people who love each other and are together, but go find other brains and bodies too. A way of being in play all the time, without repressing the other person or being repressed yourself.

But this woman – this comrade – I just can't find her, and she can't find me. And so I stay alone, with my friends, my pussies and my escapes.

Lanfranco Ponziani proposes, Spartaco Ghini disposes (money) and I accept. It is a one-way bet: if I score goals they will take out subscriptions to the *Quotidiano dei Lavoratori*. Two for every time I score.

Ghini really is a good guy. You can talk to him, and when he says something, that is what he will do. He has just one big defect: he's an owner, drowning in so much money it is scary. He's a leftist, more or less of the PCI, with that old way of talking that doesn't chime with being a communist boss, not even for love of the Party, at least to a communist worker.

My goal against Genoa is worth retelling. We are losing a Pruzzo to zero, a corner to us. Tinaglia playing for Curi, crosses to cut right, in the goal box. The ball bounces about a meter above the ground, Rosato, Rossetti, and Mosti are there; I twist in the air, and hit it right on my temple, hoping beyond hope. The ball right at the intersection, heading north, covered in mold.

If reincarnations works, I must have a Nazi soul, or maybe something even further down. It takes me over when I am not well; beyond my body which loses whole dimensions, with enormous fingers and toes, a tiny little head, it takes me over like a sense of remorse, something terrible I can't undo; I feel like I am responsible for having killed millions of people, without warning, erased from the world because of me. And I don't understand how, nor where. The terrible weight of all those bodies on me, the frightening sense of impotence later.

To me it is a criminal hooked on a fishing line, that has inserted himself inside me and takes advantage of illnesses or microbes to come back to come back to life; every time he leaves me with that stain on my brain and in my appearance.

Is this the reason I fell in love with a fascist? I thought that fascists were all ugly, ignorant and smelly. This one, not at all. With Grazia it's like being with a comrade: immediate harmony, words that mean what they say, and the dirty looks too.

We understand each other.

So what's the difference? When we talk about politics, certainly. But there must be something contrarian in us, in the way we are, how we act, how we think, and I haven't figured out what it is yet.

I know she's fascist, because they told me so, because she told me, because she told me that Potere Operaio almost got her with a Molotov, in an MSI office. But no particular odor comes from her, with her I feel myself at ease. How long had it been since anyone could get all those other pussy flies off of me? I know. There's no tomorrow. There's nothing for us, even if she told me she has already been with other comrades. It's me that isn't into this. That I get pissed off about this woman, whom I get along absurdly well with. It will end up with me leaving her here, half of her with the Duce, half with the Fascio, ok? But until then?

First I want to hear what she is telling me; how the fuck she thinks, how she is. I want to understand at what point we started toward such different places.

Is it possible to end up being famous without doing anything to become famous? Apparently so. I am becoming famous because wait for it…wait for it: because I am "involved in politics." I don't mean I am a full-blooded activist, or leader of the people. No. Just "he is interested in" or "he is involved in" politics.

Also because in the Summer I go to the labor camps. Also because I lived in a commune. Also because "he gives a raised fist salute on the pitch." In short, from that obscure unassuming bicycle rider I have become "the ultra-red footballer," "the comrade center-forward," "the left (closed) fist of God."

How do you keep all this under control? Just keep moving forward, is the first answer. Thousands of people are politically active, go to the labor camps, and live in communes. If people are shocked that a footballer does these things, it's because the world of football is behind with respect to the real world.

The world of football also includes the journalists who discover the communist footballer and put him in a cage made of newspaper lines: here, take a look at the phenomenon, and after you have looked at it, don't worry too much, the other footballers aren't like him.

I'm in all the newspapers, rightly and wrongly. What do you do with this fame? The only thing to do is to use it to say the three or four things that I have in my head, about sports, about politics, about alternative ways to live. I sure don't want to be a prophet, or act the little professor. I am simply one of the few, among those who think like me, to have access to everything, including the toilet tissue newspapers. So I am going to try to use this space to cause some trouble. Even if it's difficult, because nothing is easier for a journalist than to change the meaning of whatever you said. But if I go on TV or radio, I want to see if I will say is what I wanted to say or not.

Serie A. It makes me laugh a little. I have played in every league there is, from the promotion league on up. From fields that are tilted on an incline, to those in the middle of wolves, to those that if you're lucky they only spit at you, to those where you "have to" lose. And now here, untalented as ever, in first place in Serie B.

I still don't know how to stop, even if on the whole, I'm doing fine. I run. I neutralize my plaster feet by focusing on whoever's running behind me. I score some goals, I help the team, I have fun.

For someone who was supposed to die in the fourth Serie, it is more than enough. Of course, calling Grazia and afterward cutting out newspaper articles on why the MSI should be outlawed doesn't make a lot of sense.

Instead Andrea is stuck with the doe-eyed Claudia. I'm happy for him. It's thanks to the underwear. One day he looked at her, dirty-minded as usual. "As soon as I do a woman, I have to acquire her." So our gift to them "…with the hope that it is a dialectical thing, that one attracts the other…." And Claudia brought the underwear. Tempora mutand…

My dear comrades that have fallen in love, for us there is a need for extra-large underwear.

If one of my friends said that he was with a fascist woman, I would tell him to tell her to go fuck herself.

If I look like a fool to her on the television news, it's okay, but being embarrassed by my own party newspaper, no. The article in the *Quotidiano* is by one of those shameless people: it's a big triumphalist pumped up thing about the comrade centre-forward who will lead the masses to total revolution. Not even *Servire il Popolo* on its worst days could have managed to write so many stupid things all in one article.

"Calm as always in the face of fascist threats…" when instead I shit myself like everyone else does. In reality, I play the part of the idiotic activist who engages in the class struggle for two subscriptions per goal. My own newspaper has truly disappointed me.

Comrades come to see me at the team retreat. Usually they are super-embarrassed but I like it. I realize how different my relationships with other people are compared to those of other footballers. Instead of staring or autographs men and women comrades arrive who don't put up stupid artificial barriers in the middle of everything. We talk about me, about them, about for example what happened at Porto San Giorgio, so I am no longer a footballer on a retreat, germ-free, outside of the world and his own brain, but one of them, a comrade to spend an evening with, to laugh, to discuss things with, to have another place to go to.

One of these comrades is an old partisan, a friend of Ghini, old but lively, with the will to struggle as long as he lasts. He's in the PCI but he is open-minded. He is oriented toward young people and the "extras." "I only cut out the fascists, not comrades," he says. Fifty-seven years old, a knee that was fascist-ized, a look that holds your attention. I hang my personal problems on him. Just when I think they are too much, I think of him, or at least his story. Everything is everything. I realize that my worries are an imperceptible carving of my own making, for a minute or for fifteen minutes, a presumptuous rut to be in.

The point of making myself look ridiculous and taking myself down a peg is not to rid myself of problems and responsibilities, but instead so as to cut my umbilical obsession. To stop making the beginning and end of the world the belly button of my brain.

De-virginized television-wise as well. A program for the show "Dribbling" with Gaio Fratini, a nice guy, with poetry in his facial wrinkles, lively.

I play the actor, clumsy as a seal. This thing of playing celebrities is definitely beyond my range. For good or ill.

Good because I say what I think, using the various rotten methods of television. Ill because everything can turn to shit.

Speaking of which, a big ass fight with Mariangela. Mother and Father, it's logical they would want the celebrity son without any complications; playing football, without having to hear about me breaking people's balls.

But my sister says my words always get taken out of context and used, so it's not good that I talk. Jesus Christ, aside from the stab in the back, having been portrayed as a baboon, by *Quotidiano* itself, I couldn't give a shit what the other news agencies say about me. If other parasite journalists want to jerk themselves off by copying from the article by Giani Mura, that's not my problem.

She says, "But that article in *Settimanale*...." But screw the article in *Settimanale*, what am I supposed to do? Get a rubber and erase all the articles in all the newspapers in Italy? And besides, what do I care? If somebody buys *Il Settimanale* they aren't buying a fascist newspaper by accident. It would be as if *Secolo d'Italia* did an article and treated me badly. *Secolo d'Italia* is read by fascists.

I only have to keep saying what I think, without making too many mistakes. I just have to be myself, be as I really am, without hiding or camouflage, able to show my weaknesses as strengths. Calm. Serene. The only way to not step on your own tail is to not have one.

They ask me why I wrote "Bentista" on the doorbell. For laughs obviously. But also because no one ever blew my mind the way she did, in its most hidden and crazy corners. Not with anyone else have I ever been able to be so honest, embarrassed, ridiculous, with my throat scraped with emotion, but without hiding myself, letting the frowns show, and not just the smiles.

I remember that morning at Odense, her house near the train station, the wooden stairs that creaked more than I did. And there we are in the bedroom, under the roof, with the woods in front of us. She turns me around, uses her eyes like chisels, caresses me.

Me, squatting on the ground, Bob Dylan and Johnny Cash singing "Girl from the North Country" together, she glides over me. She kisses me first with her lips, then with her tongue, saliva and all. And she keeps turning. So as to not lose my hold I keep turning too: it's a really long kiss, so sweet and tragic. We stay in each other's mouths until we get cramps. Then I feel everything shaking. Is it possible that this Danish woman can do so much damage? But it's just the train passing below the house, making everything vibrate, us, our kiss, the windows that make noise as they shake. We look at each other and we laugh. I stick my tongue in her ear, I think that they are kind of dirty, and the German arrives.

She had been with the German the night before. I came to her the next day, bleeding, practically menstrual. "You've come to confuse things." No, I'm leaving, the confusion is in my own head, in my bones; snake's blood in my veins.

From that moment, the desire to return there is like Ariadne's thread. An emotional ball of yarn that unrolls itself, but that begins with her.

You steal the north
I'll take care of the south
And we will get ourselves there;
the compass
won't get it done: there will still be
east
And west
to argue in the birds
like the arms
of a scarecrow
without any strength
nor bones
nor flesh
to tell us the way.

One evening fear. Fear of this notoriety, of saying things that get taken to mean something else, of being the anti-celebrity only in order to be even more of a celebrity. Of being the mediocre footballer who tries to emerge from a different path; of not being understood either by the right or by the left.

Of making enemies beyond the usual ones.

I was scared; I felt rifled by all the different hardships. Maybe it was the dark; maybe I was sleeping. Now it makes me laugh to think of it. I manage my own accounts with myself pretty well; this is what I always wanted: sport that isn't only sport, and no hiding what you really think, ever.

And enemies, you know, are man's best friend.

I was also afraid of the fascists. What if they decide to get me. To beat me up, to break my leg. If they ambush me, I'll have no choice but to take them on.

I can't do anything about it, neither foresee it nor prevent it. Just wait for it to happen to me. And be afraid.

This doesn't impede anything. Fear never does. It's like before going up into the mountains. I see myself slipping and breaking something, losing my grip, avalanches falling on me. Then I go and nothing happens. Partly out of spite, partly because I am half Indian and both of these protect me. Let's hope it works with the fascists.

But this fear has another origin too: I find myself going through this thirty years after the partisan comrades got rid of them. All those dead and we still have to deal with these pieces of shit today. The Resistance is really a yellowing postcard from another time. If I take them on, some militant antifascism would be useful, so would de-anarchist-izing myself even more, and who knows, maybe some poetry would help too.

A woman writes from Rome, "I'd like to meet you," and explains that she read something about me, that she is a feminist, to not mistake her as a dick-seeking monkey, that she has a man, that she is doing fine. And that if I am interested, to contact her through an announcement in the *Messaggero*, February 11th issue, the day of her birthday. I titled the message "For feminist, complicated, cursed and without an address: down with birthdays." But it didn't get published.

Down with birthdays. My best one was three years ago, when I realized it had happened only the next day. I have never celebrated them, like Christmases, Easters, and the other holidays decided by others. I celebrate May Day, and the 25th of April, and that's it. And in any case the past two years, while I was thinking of anything but that, someone came along and ruined my day my giving me birthday greetings.

Even Maria ruins things for me. Calls that she isn't coming because she can't communicate anymore. She's afraid, maybe she isn't sure what to say to me. She says she'll write me.

It's strange how with her, who flowered in Turin, now far away geographically and unknown, I feel sure of having a future.

Three phone calls to a police commissioner of Emilia-Romagna saying that Sollier will be kidnapped by fascists. Anonymous of course. Ramaccioni tells me after the match, "You had a bodyguard all afternoon. Watch out in Perugia."

Watch out for what?

First of all I think this is fans, probably fascist ones, who want to break my balls. Secondly, the right wingers must have more important targets than me, otherwise they are really cretins (but on the other hand if they weren't cretins, they wouldn't be fascists). Thirdly, if they really want to kidnap me there isn't much I can do about it.

Or should I carry around a pistol and play cops and robbers? Or start thinking of myself as a hunted dog?

They can kidnap me, place a bomb somewhere, they can do whatever passes through their square heads. But I am certainly not going to shut myself up in my house. Why give them the satisfaction of asking myself what they want?

That's their problem.

How funny, trying to imagine the centre-backward rat, my first thought is: contact lenses. That I won't have the container for them and I'll have to throw them out. It's really true that the greatest events depend on the smallest things.

He's an enemy of mine. If I play poorly then I play poorly all the same. But this isn't one of those enemies that declare themselves openly, no this is a an underground enemy. A cross between worms and ostriches. Wallowing in the mud. Stripping. Getting drunk in every puddle. Then sticking his head back under the ground to take shelter. What can I say, it's the right place to look for the grains of sand that make up his brain. But he looks ridiculous with his ass up sticking up out of the ground. And it makes it too easy to kick him in the ass.

Poor guy, his name is Ricci. He writes for the *Nazione*. There's another that writes for *Stadio*, Cesare Trentino. This guy sees a footballer with long hair and immediately says he's worthless. If he's also a communist, then he is always the worst player on the field. This wordsmith is probably one of those that think that sport doesn't mix with politics. Openly. But if you need someone working down in the dirt, don't worry, he's got it. They tell me he's old, so at least you only have to put up with him for a little longer.

Journalists, one day I'll make up my own classification. I will count from one to ten and then I will be mean.

The raised fist started by accident. A salute to other comrades, a little sign of complicity, nothing more. It wasn't a campaign rally, nor propaganda, nor any other various shit. An instinctive gesture, that they are ruining for me, a fist that they are ripping right out of my hands. A whole bunch of things have been attached to it that don't belong there, imaginary discourses, invented proclamations, struggles over illustrated magazines. And they all buzz like flies, hit their heads, and die. A fist full of flies is the meaning they have searched for in my raised fist salute. If somebody gets upset because communists salute each other with a raised fist, then that's their own problem, and their own fears.

The latest fascist stuff. A noted thug sees a poster of the Perugia team in a bar, sees me, and threatens, "If you don't take that piece of shit down from there, I will come back with others and we will tear down the bar." Obvious, the poster disappears.

Then a guy who looks like me gets beaten up and insulted: Damned red bastard and so on, with threats. He defends himself repeating "It's not me."

I've always wondered what the effect is of receiving mail from people you don't know. I read a lot about footballers drowning in a sea of letters. Male and female admirers, more admirers, and fans, and more fans. I asked myself what someone could say to Riva who didn't know him, beyond having seen him in underpants behind a football. What can they tell him except that he's handsome, and they would be happy to fuck him, and to score a lot of goals?

I interrogated myself, in my little brain, on my own reactions. It is true that I am a much more minor figure than Riva, and much uglier, but what if notwithstanding all this they still write me a bunch of bullshit? Throw them in the toilet? Or do I answer them, attacking?

None of the above. Even the question of answering letters depends on what kind of person you are, and how you live. A kind of natural selection put in motion by previous decisions. In fact none of them are frivolous letters. On the contrary. The write to me from the prisons, and from strange places where they make poetry.

Franco Rapanelli, called Minini, incarcerated, four months still to go. He writes of friendship, of human warmth, of anger that turns into a struggle to change things, "…and when we are done, no one will any longer write from these places."

Tommaso di Ciaula, a drill-press operator and poet, sends me a copy of his book, *Chiodi e rose*, which is beautiful.

And Rina Dal Zilio, a nurse in Treviso. She also bandages together poetry, but the kind that doesn't do much healing.

Then young girls write to ask me how to start being involved in politics and with whom; how to run away from home and not have to return, brought back by carabinieri.

Naturally I refuse to play the game of giving advice. At most I give some technical information. And then it is up to you to handle things in the best way you can. Again, here too, not out of lack of concern but out of real concern.

In the end, there is no way out of it, everything is sex. We lose at home to SPAL, ridiculously, playing awfully. And granting the criticisms, and leaving aside the fact that we are still in first place, what does the *dolce vita* have to do with it? No one even remembers Fellini anymore, but the *dolce vita* has come back into fashion. The players don't do well? Of course not, because they fuck from morning to night: whoremongers, nothing more, the lot of them.

If this sexological spite was found in *Gente* or some piece of crap like that, we could understand; but I read this stuff in *Paese Sera*. Amenta, Marchei, and Sollier are the principle defendants accused, and they're condemned to be publicly castrated. There's no middle ground here, a footballer can't be ill, have some problems, be out of shape, have a bad day. None of this is allowed. The theory of the dick provides an answer to everything.

Certainly aside from the damage it does, it's silly. With a groin full of rust, what feel like continuous stab wounds up the ass, my whole right side's a disaster; my balls feel like they're being squeezed from the knee up to the belly button, the pain's killing me; the groin pain alone makes my dick to go limp just from the thought of fucking. And yet they tell me that I am filling up pussies repeatedly, like a necklace. So many pearls, stringing them on my dick, one after the other. To think that at the moment my dick feels like its hanging by a thread. Yet I'm living the *dolce vita*.

I've started nicknaming the journalist Enzo D'Orsi "Novella 2000." He's earned it.

But talking about sex in a serious way? It's bad for you, it's good for you. Is it really such a back-breaker as they say it is? I don't know. Certainly if one spends the whole night fucking, then fucks some more, they aren't being athletic. But if one ejaculates the right amount, and then sleeps at night, no problem.

The right amount differs from body to body; on one's habits, on the time period. I for example have to fuck once a week. Twice in the really happy moments. Not because I have to squeeze it out physically, but for dealing with aggressiveness. The game I play needs it. I always have to play at a super-rhythm; in a slow-moving match I am pretty useless. And flirting cheers me up, and calms me down. It takes away from me the desire to jump on top of the ball, to hip check my adversary, to be too aggressive. So I become a calmer player with legs of wood, with the obvious results.

But be careful also of the opposite, that is, fucking too little. You feel full of energy, ready to break everything, and so you aren't able to do anything. The fact is being super-full of energy is neutralized by counteracting forces. Such as, you have so much energy that you are making up your own headlines, inside yourself, with excess energy. You feel like you're going to explode, but at the same time you're nervous, tense, irritable, with the result that all that energy ends up creating internal thunderstorms. All because you didn't use that contraption you have between your legs, so that the thunderstorms could get sent to your brain to recharge the battery. That's all.

Then it depends on whether you have an ongoing relationship that stabilizes your sex life, or whether you take it as it comes, which means that there are periods of fireworks, and then periods of absolute chastity. I'm one of the latter.

Which leads me to bring up again the question of jerking off. I don't give a damn about fucking just to fuck. To park it somewhere for a while and nothing else. I want to be with someone that I want to go to bed with and also go with others. If that's not there, then rather than use someone's body like a sex machine, I use my hand – expertly – and it continues to be a way of getting to know myself.

Manuela, formerly a right wing "qualunquista" and now in perennial leftward-migration. She confessed to having an abortion, joined a union, stopped crying. Now she no longer says things like, "You can tell you have never been in love." Now she has had enough of suffering for a man. Now she could live in a commune. We managed to pull off having sex. First uncomfortably, circling each other, almost as if studying the enemy. Then a savage, liberating assault. Our sterilized friendship wiped away in one fell swoop. Fuck words.

Sex is always the last battle. When you come out of your hiding place, rendering naked your last defenses, ones that have survived through years of friendship.

All friends should make love at least once. Find the holes inside, tremble together.

It's useless. You can't be an activist like this. One minute you are and the next you're not. Always catching up, asking about what's happened, trying to get squared away. And then you leave to go on retreat, probably when there is something important coming up.

This isn't activism, it's alibi. The other hand? Maybe finding a way to use football as a political terrain, otherwise I will always end up being expropriated, forced to act politically outside of the contradictions that I live every day. It's absurd. And in this way, the whole time engaged in sports ends up being wasted, confined within limits that made it impossible to work on changing it. I think that sports are an important field to be active in. One which the left has always avoided because of a question of priorities, but also because of its own inability.

It was like that for music until a little while ago. If you talked about a concert or a poem, or how songs were important, you were considered a hippy. Namely a useless race, bastard flower children. Meanwhile, "politics" narrowly speaking was a serious thing.

Now, fortunately, they've come to realize – we've come to realize – that the cultural areas are as important as the political ones, are political. And so parties, concerts, musical criticism, alternative music, etc.

It probably works the same way for sports. Maybe my job is to contribute to accelerating this process, even given the cultural desert weighing down the extraleft in this field.

Why does every article about sports in *Quotidiano*, but also in *Il Manifesto* and in *Lotta Continua* makes you laugh your guts out? I think it's because beyond the generic slogan "let's take over sports," the comrades have no idea how to go about it. They've never worried about it. Instead, sport, for those who practice it (few), those who cheer for their teams (too many), and those who have to put up with it, concerns everyone.

Therefore, we have to say that it belongs to everyone, and that every neighborhood has to have equipment available to work up a sweat, to improve your health, to have fun playing with. But we also need to start thinking about how to get there; how to get down from the high horse of rhetoric, how to practically get our hands on these damned sports.

The UISP does have something to say. But in between saying and doing there is....the PCI. Good resolutions are one thing. Another is to have the red city councils still stick to the previous party line: money for the important sports, that is the professional ones, and crumbs for the alternative sports. It should be exactly the opposite.

In any case, lacking a sports plan on the part of Avanguardia Operaia, I have to organize myself to struggle alone; I'll be alongside the UISP when it does what it says it will do. In other words, I will make myself available.

It certainly isn't pleasant to be in a political organization and to have to have to handle things by yourself. Also because these people are political retards, and they end up paying a political price.

Giancarlo "Zumbo" Raffaeli is my teammate and friend. Communist, but in the PCI, with a face that looks Moroccan, from Foligno, "lu centru de lu munnu." We're friends, even if we will end up far apart. He is somewhat the prototypical Communist by proxy, for changing things but not too much, for tradition at all costs.

He lives a more or less planned-out life in fact. He's getting married soon, in a while he will buy a house, he will keep voting for the PCI, continue to believe in it but not do anything. And he will continue to not create alternative ways of living and thinking. He stays there, already a bit aged, ready to consume things he already knows. He doesn't venture off the beaten path.

But it's nice enough hanging out with him. Another is Walter Sabatini, the total opposite. He's not a comrade, but he lives life as it comes, in the moment, without too many blinders.

If only it were possible to merge the two into one person…

Thanks to them the retreats are not as boring. We reinvent the games we played when we were children. Hide and seek, blind man's bluff, etc. It's our way of disguising our desperation with the retreat. You have to get through two days with minimal damage. Some play cards, but it's not much of a solution, and television is a worse one.

Someone says you can read. But you can't. This is what really sucks about the retreat: you can't read or write or concentrate on anything. It's a form of intellectual impotence during which a normal page of an ordinary book turns your brain to mush. Try and write, and out of the mush come postcard-quality sentences.

I've never felt myself to be so stupid and incapable as I do on Saturdays. It seemed like every drop of my intelligence, of my will power, of my imagination has dried up, and commits suicide just thinking about tomorrow's match.

And that's how the games were born. And they're fun too. What sucks is having to play them out of the lack of anything else to do and not out of having chosen freely. An evening spent playing may horrify those who are "mature," but this is the maturity of mushrooms, which immediately start to smell when they go bad.

You always have to make it rain. And not shelter yourself from it. Learn to hate mental umbrellas. Avoid saying and telling yourself that there are certain things you only do up to a certain age, then you start doing other things, and then others still later. You have to refuse these guardhouses, these psychological tollbooths. You can do everything, and when you want to. All that matters is not imprisoning yourself. Be serious, mature, true; but also crazy, childlike, and able to play. Ready to struggle, decide, live; but also to dab your eyes with a tissue and to seek out others.

Otherwise there is the risk of a much worse blind man's bluff, lacking playfulness, just being sad. And then you never get to catch anyone.

About Maria. About how we were together. About her body, her thoughts, her messes, her laugh, inhabit perfectly my theory of living without permanent couples. She came and left like a pleasant flash of lightning, like a strong handshake, like a string of saliva.

Why should I be surprised? Or make believe I am? I "knew" it was like this with her; and she knew the same about me. We stayed away out of fear, or scarcity, or who knows what. We were within range of each other's nerves, however.

We were man and woman, friends and lovers, feminist and male chauvinist, octopus and squid. Our tentacles free to go where they wanted.

On the doorbell it says "Feminist" too. Since a man can be one too, of course; without having ever menstruated, or had an abortion, or having feared getting pregnant, without ever having been a housewife.

And I was one even when I didn't know I was one. When I was little and I got pissed off because we couldn't all play together, boys and girls; when the girls couldn't go out in the evening because they were girls; when I asked how come someone who got pregnant was a whore, but the guy was a conquistador; when I stopped to think that that menstruation was really inconvenient and I uselessly searched my own body for a corresponding pattern. Etcetera.

Now I feel "feminist" because I feel that it concerns me. I certainly don't think that everything can be reduced to being comrades and then everything is all fixed up. I know too many comrades who are politically great but who are real shits in interpersonal relationships; completely unable to break through the shell; who think of women as sexual playthings, or as little more than that.

Nor do I think that women are always right and we are always wrong. We know that we men have and defend all kinds of privileges, power, and inequality. And that women are right to hit us on the heads about it.

I volunteer my head, messed up as it is, and make it available, but I don't want to suffer for historical vendettas like, "You have oppressed us for so long, now it's our turn." Precisely because I believe in feminism. Besides, saying that men are all assholes doesn't help anyone. Women have to distinguish between who is alright and who isn't; and who is into it only out of opportunism or because it's in fashion, and it doesn't take much to figure that out.

As for myself, seeing as how I wash the dishes, prepare meals, clean the floor, do the grocery shopping, live as a house-man, I feel like on the domestic side I am pretty sheltered from criticism. The sexual side however is open to question, even if I am not able to be a dominator in bed, and if I never have thought of my dick as the center of the universe. Still, I have my good dose of aggressiveness, my being closed up, my layers of crust. Someone got me over Bente, others did the same for Maria. But layers of crust, like microbes and privileges, reproduce. You can't stop them.

This is the great merit of feminism. It doesn't give you any peace. It is a constant opening to question.

Angelino Caporali, stabbed with a fascist knife, right in the center of Perugia. He's in the hospital, more dead than alive, hanging on to his knifed guts. The killer this time is called Radoni and naturally he escaped.

The same evening, a big fight at the headquarters of the MSI, me finally on the front lines, a meter from the door. But of course the real front line is elsewhere: some little street further down ten Molotovs are thrown into the headquarters of the FUAN. The whole place burns. And it is not even illegal. Do we or don't we have a Constitution that prohibits the reconstruction of the Fascist Party and related groups?

The only thing that would make things worse would be if I ran for office. Aside from the fact that I don't vote very often, it is not a good idea to mix athletic notoriety and political aspirations. If one day I ever did run, it would be with a real, genuine everyday political relationship with the people who supported me. It would have to be after we had done real mass work, and only if I represented something concrete in the struggle. And certainly not to steal some votes from the stadium.

This is my – our – way of doing politics. Exactly because I believe in a different kind of relationship than our office-holders, including the communists in the PCI. And because you get things out of political credibility, not out of some stupid fandom.

This idea of proposing instead of having an answer is really right. In any story, a book, a movie, in whatever, healing the wound doesn't count for much (that is, the "cure" of the author, of the party, of the party "line"), but instead delve into it, explore it, be the guide for anyone who wants to get involved. The cure, the solution, the answer, people can then go looking for.

What need is there for these ideological reins, for this obligatory training. Isn't it a way of seeing others as intellectual mendicants?

Everyone should be free to adjust the blinders as they wish, according to their conscience, their character, and the weaknesses they find. What need is there to make someone always and at any cost chase a cultural carrot, an answer, a way out found by whoever is assisting them? Are they donkeys?

Isn't it really the fear of other answers, of other paths, of "other" that is frightening? Why package a "finished" product, something with its question, its answer, its line?

Isn't it preferable to merely be provocative, letting the interlocutor interrogate themselves to see if the argument makes sense to them?

Piero is right, why be afraid of "mistreating" the Resistance? Why not set up for the thirtieth anniversary a series of interviews showing that the Resistance just gets its tits whipped? Whoever listens will be perfectly capable of knowing how tits should be, and who it is that has milked them, and why.

Otherwise we end up going around in the usual circles. So then people see everything already resolved and pre-package by other brains, other ways of thinking, and they end up repressing any criticism, fantasy, or imagination.

Instead no. Get up off your ass and listen in, then pull yourself away, and everyone replies in the way they know how. And even if all they talk about is the barber, then it's a great result.

It's the same as with the children who ask for autographs. Do I owe them my explanation? I can give it to them, but isn't it better if they try to find their own explanation, so that my refusal is just a simple breakdown in the mechanism, and they find out how to adjust it themselves?

To celebrate the Resistance, I finally asked my father about that train that deported people to Porta Nuova. And what it was like to be with the partisans. He happened to be near the train by accident, and happened to have a loaf of bread that immediately disappeared in a sea of hands. With the partisans in part for adventure, in part out of fear that if he returned to Turin to work he might find himself on the wrong part of that train. Then he told me about a couple of missions.

The voyage through the Val di Susa, the platoon in camouflage, using the voice of one of them that spoke German, stealing two motors, some munitions and some petrol. Stealing hand grenades in front of the Church in Chiomonte. They took away three truck chassis, before the guards ever noticed. Then he told me about his first rifle, a 91, found in a ditch, thrown away by a deserting soldier. He hid it in a vineyard; when the time came to try it out he was afraid it would explode because it was full of soil, so he tied a metal wire to the trigger and fired it from far away.

I like these things for their non-exceptional character. They were everyday things, normal, they belonged to the common man. How they managed to do these things and remain such; and not be propelled by the war into a more reactive mentality, more extremist, I don't know. The drama is over. It made them do incredible things, crazy, without limits, and it left them as though behind them there was a stonecutter: lined up, jammed together one right after the other, paving stones to the so-called new world. Is it possible that that wedge of pain, of tragedy, of desperation, was only passed from one to another just once, and never has to be again?

The guts of Angelino held together okay. How is it being stabbed comrade? "I almost didn't notice it, I only felt something really cold inside my warm guts, then the pain started, this thick blood started flowing out. And I stood there like a fool, standing up, with my hands against the hole."

For everyone who gets out of jail, another one enters. They charged Stefano for the Molotovs. Someone says they saw him hide a bag full of bottles. Naturally the would-be killer Radoni is still at large.

My little obscenity came to see me and talk her shit. There are those who are better and those who are not as good. Those who are better naturally must dominate over the others. There has to be someone who thinks and decides for the masses because they are all sheep. Almirante is exceptional: fascism is revolutionary.

In short, the supermen with their superbrains, and she, the superbitch that repeats this shit to me. The choice was certainly not hard to make, namely, fuck you. We didn't touch each other. I felt like an old Indian, with the enemy in my tipi, with them protected by the most ferocious sort of hospitality. Maybe it would have been normal to fuck, to burn off all our mud in our sexual brook and then say ciao. But I am worse than a Trappist monk when it comes to these things.

Why in the world should going to bed bring together apples and oranges? I have never believed in a love that fixes everything in the world, that overcomes barriers and distances, that draws a line for you. So forget about me thinking that jumping between those thighs a couple of times can bandage up this romantic disaster.

An old Indian. Hospitality is sacred, and so is war. So I watched her leave. Once I had made up my mind, everything was all right. Like letting loose a landslide. It just takes a second. Then you get overwhelmed and everything is all right. The dogs find you, bitten by the stones with sand for saliva. You're safe now, and it's all over.

Two girls with a banner, a demonstration for the comrades who've been killed; to be sad, and pissed off, and yet at the same time to have the desire to live, to see two nice banner-holders, Black-Hair and Golden Eyes; I don't even remember what was written on the banner, I listen to people talking about the killed comrades, hear them close with the lie that they are still with us.

Instead they are not with us anymore. And they can't struggle anymore, can't live, or love, or have a stomach ache. They took them away from us, with bullets and truckloads. This teaches us something, but does not console us. Black Hair and Golden Eyes console us, but they don't teach us.

It's true. There's nothing easier to do today than join the PCI. They give you a line, protection, organization, and there's no problem. You don't have to change your life, nor make anyone else change theirs. Sign the membership card and give them your vote, and the party machine will do the rest. You go where they take you.

Those who talk about the tanks in Prague to use them against the PCI (which in any case condemned them) make me laugh. So do those who accuse them of being Russia-philes. The most dangerous tanks are actually the intellectual ones. They are a monstrous proxy machine, they are the sections where the only debate is over confirming the party line; they are the invention of the "Historic Compromise," the wish to use the petrol of the Christian Democrats, which is adulterated with sugar and sand, in order to make the people's car go. Nothing could be more absurd. If the DC has a popular soul, you will find it in concrete programs, in struggle, certainly not by holding hands with the putrefied ministers of a government that's falling apart.

All this many comrades in the PCI know, even if they don't admit it, and yet they defend the decisions of their leadership. I don't agree, but they armored-combat-vehicle-ize their brains and they keep going back. In any case the Party never errs, the Party is always right, the Party is far-seeing, the Party is Godlike, and at this point, we have decapitated ourselves.

Is the Party the opium of the people?

A match in Palermo, zerotozero, then one in Avellino. In between a week of retreat at Cava dei Tirreni. On the free Monday some rest, some go to Naples, some go to whores. And some rediscover the pleasure of hitchhiking.

I leave that morning and return that evening, exhausted. I get as far as Paestum, looking around the ruins, and remembering my own, with Giovanna, many years ago. I eat, I remember, I walk.

Someone stops me and tells me we will win on Sunday, and that I will score a goal. And he says he means it because his name is Miracolo. I return to Cava in a coach as if in a Western, then five days of absolute boredom, and then, the last evening, Santa. I see her for ten minutes, not more, but she takes me by the throat, and I feel like the thought of not seeing her ever again is suffocating. She is a lump in the brain, a fly that swims in my blood, against the current. A nerve that's gone mad.

When I go, this date is tattooed on me, I'm scarred by the desire to be in bed with her.

We really do win the match and I really do score a goal and it really is a miracle. It is the week that Walter's misfortune hits bottom. He was supposed to play, then, training for the Nationals, a twisted ankle, a cast, and my reentry.

Is it possible after everything else that two friends have to compete over getting to wear one jersey between them?

I keep not knowing how to act with a mendicant. Alms no, because I hate that. Talking no, because it doesn't lead to anything; insulting God and society and destiny serves no purpose. I pass, measure impotence by side glances, and I pull myself away, with difficulty, distancing myself fifty meters.

Maria plays with being a flower child. She comes to see me by surprise, in a hurry, round trip and pointlessly. I am on some football field. She leaves me a note and a kaleidoscope.

So there's nothing for me to do but read it, curse and look for her through the window. Naturally without result. I need a porn-erotic kaleidoscope, her all in pieces, each brightly colored. And then she recomposes herself before my eyes, I just have to turn the scope, and she undresses, opens her legs, trips over the light, she rolls me over pecking me with her mouth, pieces of glass like razors in my veins, a sweet hemorrhage, an ejaculation of thoughts, her back raked by finger nails, sharp specks of sweat, her eyes scratched with my bullshit.

A porn-erotic fantasy, rather than a kaleidoscopic one.

Almirante came to town; the duce of words himself, the emperor of the fine phrase, the elastic jockstrap of the old fuckers that go hear him.

He is convincing enough when he says that we have to be real men, with hard balls. Balls he has. He had a hundred of them, all with their heads shaved, outside and inside, eyes fixed like boiled eggs, club-members by profession.

Loaded up on the buses, and transported here and there around Italy, so as to make it look like there are a lot of them, like Mussolini did with his tanks, to defend the head prick, jockstraps for the head, nostalgic old droolers, held together by the force of creams.

We heard that there were about forty people there, like mummies, and we were there too. In between were the cops. The usual commissioner and vice-commissioner, who wouldn't dream about missing even one of these things.

The attack was not planned. A couple of hours earlier, Pietro Conti had spoken in the same hall – the Sala dei Notari – and it would have been enough if he had just "talked" some more, in other words if we had occupied the piazza, the comrades of the PCI, us, every real antifascist, and so the little gorilla, where could he have put himself? He would have run away like he did so many times before.

Instead, the PCI said no, because the election campaign is sacred. Then, if you accuse them of having been domesticated, they reply asking us what do we know, they have had their own people killed. And no one suspects that they are messing with us, talking about those deaths, that having struggled hard in the past is an excuse for not doing so today. In fact, some of the comrades of the PCI who came to hear Conti stay with us to wait till the *ducis* finishes. Not to attack him, but to make him feel the elbow in his side at least.

In the meantime, the commissioners-vice-commissioners continue to push us down Corso Vanucci. Two meters behind them the idiots with boiled eggs for brains decide to catch flies with their "Roman salute." No one stops them. The cops must be so used to seeing their superiors guilty of giving the fascists salute that they don't even notice.

The rifleman finishes his fireworks, and then leaves. It should all be over, but one commissioner loses that little bit of his head that he still had attached. He orders a charge on the steps, a place of peace, pigeons, and music. People falling, batons, guerilla combat. It seems like winter, with drops of rain mixed with fog. But it is summer, the fog is teargas, and we have to suck lemons yet again. All because of some imbecilic commissioner. The one positive thing is seeing Angelino, healthy again, with his stitches still fresh and his guts a bit shorter now. And Stefano is there too, on parole for the Molotovs. They gave him a year and a half. When it is comrades in the dock, they make sure it gets done quickly and done well.

Perugia-Genoa 1-2; Atalanta-Perugia 2-1; Perugia-Sambenedettese 1-2; Verona-Perugia 0-2; Pescara-Perugia 1-1; Perugia-Novara 1-0.

Or, how you go in six weeks from head of the class to shitheads, to promotion. We lose three matches in a row and already they have given us up for dead. Perugia, baked in the sun, the Griffin stumbles over the line, end of a dream. And here come the criticisms of Giorgio Molini because he prepared us badly. The blows for Castagner because he didn't change the formation. Ilario loses his head and before the match with Sambenedettese he takes us on retreat until Wednesday. And never was the point of a retreat more lost in the result. Nervous as electric wires we even manage to lose that match too.

Then Verona. We leave Friday, as usual. Retreat at Sirmione, but more than footballers on retreat, we seem like tourists. Two days to eat ice cream, cherries, peaches, and strawberries, with Zumbo, Gert, Cefalo, and Tondino. Naturally, we also play hide and seek. Cefalo and Gert keep low, and Zumbo and I hide behind a big door. Some time passes and the door moves, and the two of us, trying to play dead, attempt to close it again. Push here, push there, a suicidal hand fits itself inside the space between the two parts of the door.

One more push and the human sandwich is consumed. Then we wonder: this poor finger doesn't seem too familiar after all. We open the door and a fortyish man is massaging the slice of salami. Sorry, we tell him, we were playing hide and seek. A little ways away, our two friends are cracking up with laughter. "Get out of here" the little man says with all the hatred he could muster in his voice. We run away with our faces distorted as we try not to laugh.

We end up in the park with Francesco Ghini, who is evidently not related to Indians or to pioneers because he has kept low the whole time.

Instead, Sunday it's Verona that keeps low. One of our best matches. Their own fans even cheer us on, two goals by Gert, one with co-ownership with Giacomi, our nightmare kicked in the ass. But just the Sunday before we were a disaster, and yet no retreat. So? So, it means that we were not physically burnt out, but instead our brains were stressed out by the whole season in our heads, the tension, the need to score points.

We needed to shake it off, to get rid of all the insects biting us, the obituary writers, the "can they still do it?" fans. And it was probably this week of joyful play, without having to think too much, it was the strawberries that healed us psychologically, it was that hand, sandwiched between the door.

It was also the campaign rallies. For the first time I had to choose between being a footballer and playing football. I felt the strain of the moment, and I was tempted to leave aside everything that wasn't football. It was only for a week, after all. Then I realized that this was a trick that fear was playing on me, and it was time to overcome it. I continued the election campaign, with two rallies a day, eating sandwiches for dinner at midnight. It was the right way to go.

We conclude our difficult election campaign; we certainly don't lack for enemies; Proletarian Democracy feels like Fort Apache; it has to defend itself from Lotta Continua which says to vote for the PCI, and also from the PCI which says we are siphoning off votes and dividing the left, and which opening the drawbridge to the DC is worried we will leave them with only the drawbridge from the DC's "thirty years of inculcating Italians with freedom." And now, even from the weather, not the stupid daily newspaper *Tempo*, which would be normal, but the atmospheric one, that one that accuses us of being opposing extremisms, with thunder and lightning, and which rains on us and on the fascists alike.

But we defend ourselves well. Our electoral campaign is more a dialogue, a chat, a continuation of the relationship we already have with people, rather than an electoral fungus, or a pissing on the heads of anyone who listens to us. Whoever votes for us doesn't pull themselves away, doesn't use a proxy, doesn't wait for us to do it for them, but accepts the challenge to struggle alongside us, with us, to move together. We want everyone to do politics in person, and then we won't need to talk anymore about bureaucracy, or about compromised leaderships, to mention only two evils.

Pescara arrives. The sacred mathematics promotes us, then everybody goes to vote. Then a week of celebrating for the two victories. And it's beautiful, even if for the communists of Perugia it seems like the more important one is the success of the team. Not much celebrating for the defeat of the Demofanfani; a mass popular explosion for our promotion to Serie A. And aside from the obvious criticisms (the Stadium-drug which works here too, choices that subordinate the sport to the elites, like a new stadium, and the same old arguments by the leftist city council), this party is fantastic.

The city looks for itself, touches itself, prepares itself, embellishes itself, embraces itself, fidgets with itself, and winds it all up with a colossal, collective, orgasm. It seems like a Medieval festival with the center of Perugia painted white and red in every possible way, on the banners, on the people, on the flags. It is a joyous anthill, enthusiastic and a lot of fun. It goes on all night.

Walter, Miguel and I out on the streets with the cry of the *curva*, "hospitality boxes, hospitality boxes, up your asses" then we perch on the stairs. Luciana is there. We met two hours ago at the restaurant. All dinner long we looked, peeked, looked into each other's eyes. As I am leaving she cuts off my path and says "Ciao, I'm Luciana." We make a date to meet.

And here we are. We laugh, we enjoy the last bits of the party, pass some drunk dressed in white and red. Before the stairs empty I have already obtained three pieces of "information" about her: she's a slut, she goes with everyone, she acts strangely…don't they know that the first commandant is mind your own fucking business?

It's getting on five o'clock in the morning, we are the only two out, the illuminated piazza, deserted, the cathedral complicit with its towers and its shadows. We talk and we kiss with our asses chilled on the cold stair. I tell her what they told me, and she curses, but not very much, almost like she was used to it. The beautiful thing is we don't know anything about each other, and this is why we look at each other with trust, two happy sluts.

But there are some at the party who are not feeling well: like that ostrich-worm Ricci, or that I-will carry-this-trying-to-forget-it-to-my-grave-Trentini. One about the team, the other about me, they had written every evil thing possible. Like perfect vultures they flew down to their carcasses. Now they have disappeared. The festive air forces them to hide, vultures on their mental covered-lurch. How awful to have to hang from the walls and to chew your own vomit. And how nice to think that they are doing badly.

In Milan, Elio is tired of studying. I remember when he arrived at my house, as contraband, having hitchhiked from Domenico. He arrived from Indochina, pouring rain; there was a plate of chips, our baptism and communion, they were more cooker than frying pan. Then all evening regaling us with the stories of his travels, telling us about strange loves, about poetry. The next day we split up on the train for Milan, in a beautiful way, and hurried. I memorized a poem of his:

The high plains is a darker strip
the sky falls at its margins
and encircles it in mystery.
They are higher than the moon
the men who on the precipice
stretch the evening.
Ancient, tasting of life,
of millenarian awaiting,
the high plains stays silent.
The sun rises behind that machine
and sets at the soldiers' base
every day.
They are carved above this mountain
the men who live here.
I, pass through these heights
– desert of fear and of wind –
like another planet.
Everything is far away
that my body gathers
like a whisper.

And I remember the opening to another poem, one of ferocious sweetness:

On every side the desert advances right up to the sky
I walk across it from afar.

In the evening when the sun will touch the horizon
I will have to spread out my sleeping bag
now ragged, on the sweetest point
and sleep...

Then Maria. Of her I remember that far away first kiss. Her tongue as it slithered around between my lips, suddenly, unexpectedly, like a foot stuck in a door to keep it from closing.

We talk forever, about everything. We see each other two, three times a year and it's as if we were traveling along the same line. Like being on a train, she looks out on one side, I out the other. We see different landscapes. Two, three times a year there's a station stop, we get out, take a walk together, she tells me about her landscape, I tell her about mine. With total honesty about the details, even those kept hidden, transgressive, "perverted."

I look at her. You know, I say, that I really don't have any desire to fuck you? And she replies: "Don't worry, I have even less, I'm tired of men."

But a touch here, a touch there, let me see, let me try this, just a lick, it all ends in an amazing joking coitus. On the other hand, whoever said that to make love you have to be serious and feeling sorry for yourself?

Traveling, the border, France. The only thing that ruins the trip for me is that fucking transfer window. I get nervous just thinking that someone is will be evaluating me for weight, goals, presence, appearances, age, cartilage, and every now and then I have to call to see if I've been sold. I hope the telephones jam.

Larzac, the farmers in revolt, fantastic and savage. Then Bordeaux after an insane voyage, flies of fatigue in my eyes, midnight. If I don't find her I might kill myself. But I do. She kisses me on the neck. Always beware of the ones that kiss you on the neck.

The next day I leave, wanting to cry. I say goodbye with my Adam's apple grating on my vocal cords, my voice coming out sounding swollen. Basically, she beat me up. Two people can't be such friends and then not say anything at all to one another, two strangers on an empty streetcar, at night, awkward, ridiculously trying to ignore each other.

And it was the most certain, tried and true, sincerely felt friendship. Two people who hitchhike together is like having been married, or so I thought, there always remains something between them.

But the old folks in my hometown had a strange saying: "being sure is death." And I finally understand.

I feel bad all over. It feels like she stuck broken glass all over me, like on some old wall, and I go around, all cut up and cutting. I leave with a wound in the middle of my brain, deep, infected; I will want it to heal up and create a scab.

With Viviane it is definitely not a "see you later." Even if she doesn't play rugby anymore, she still remembers how to tackle someone. I went down face first and I kicked her. Expelled for life. Being sure is death.

I get to Angers. A Spaniard, Joseph, an Italian and two French twins who don't look at all alike, traveling around Bretagne. A land of dreams, rebels, life. Wind that feels like sandpaper on your skin, the Bretons that if you call them French they get pissed off, your tent pitched in the middle of the sea and the next morning the sea is a kilometer away.

Bathing under the raindrops with two Finns, the waves really high, the drops of rain falling heavily. Waves that break far away, that crack, spit out all the Madonnas before they argue with the rocks. My prayer has been heard: you can't telephone out to Italy. So I stop thinking about it.

Making love to Anne Marie in a lopsided Canadian army tent; it's humid, and full of holes. My butt moving up and down at times hits the wet canvas and it gets stuck there, the sweat mixing with the water, the tent almost a bath tub, we enjoying our private rainstorm.

Then with Joseph in Paris. After ten days, I find a copy of *Tuttosport*. Lying down on the Eiffel Tower, I read that I haven't been sold to another team, that instead Agroppi, Berni, Cicottelli and Novellino are arriving. The team is more or less as it was.

I'm happy. I've met a lot of people, started a lot of relationships. To leave Perugia would suck. Almost nothing has been fully proven, or known well. Another year should cement things.

As soon as I close the newspaper, I leave Perugia for Paris. We walk all day in the middle of the anthill. So long as I don't live here, this city is the best place to come to live.

Amsterdam instead disappoints me. Too many second-hand hippies, an atmosphere of people who are world-weary, who know everything, closed up in their certainties. A lot of these young people who are burnt out and full of holes seem to me like the employees of the highway rest stops, gray, sad. Here drugs are available right on the street, every ten steps someone asks you "hashish?." And how can I explain that I don't even know how to smoke the "Nationals"?

And the women in the windows, like a kilo of apples or a side of beef. It hits you like a fist in the face. But it's certainly not any different than the women who get beaten, or used as fashion models, or as mouthpieces. Only it is more brutal and disconcerting.

Two days of bumming around, then we go our separate ways. Joseph continues on and goes to Denmark, I return to the retreat. I give him a letter for Bente, which will also serve to find him a place to sleep. And I return home.

It's been a year since I left home. Has it gone like it was supposed to? I think so. I made four good kicks, and not just in football. I proved to myself that having more money didn't have to mean becoming an imbecile; I made some of this money available to my comrades; so fuck whoever says that it's easy to say "I would give some away" when you don't have it to give. I solved my political paralysis, sending the lone wolf to the kennel. I was in the pages of the newspapers and on television screens without screwing up too much. Everybody knows me, and I know myself a little better.

On a different note, a year ago I didn't think about Gisella. She is an actress in the theatre, dark reddish hair, a nice voice, without any angles, an enveloping personality. I call her more than anything else to get rid of a stone; like taking a little pebble out of your shoe: it's little, but insistent, and it makes it hard to walk. It bruises. She treacherously tells me she desires to see me. I jump in the car and go bang my head against an entire evening of memories. Two stupid hours of laughing, joking, walking around in old socks, then ten minutes of that famous pebble. She becomes a stone, a bruise, bitter. I buzz around in my head like a suicidal mosquito, my brain springs leaks, my dreams get lame. Just what I needed, a reason to go on retreat.

She's strange. A suicide addict, with an earthquake stare. Above all, distant. I declare myself unrepentantly in love.

In Perugia my new house is waiting for me, my fourth. I hope there will be many more, with a lot of other people. This one is with Nico and Rossella, even if it is a half-hearted choice: I had talked with him about living together. She came along. They are together, I don't know her at all. So who knows. As always, the only way to find out is to try.

Even in football the house is different. Without Ghini Perugia has taken the old road. It could have been an organization open to the participation of the fans, even with the players as co-managers. Instead it has fallen in line with the others. A vertical company with White Pen at the top. Then the board, the sports director, and so on down. The fans have to root and that's all. For Ghini instead, these "minority shareholders" (the famous swindle shares) were to elect representatives to the board, with decision-making powers. "Then the board and the President themselves should risk a little more from their own pockets. Hopefully making money, but risking something. Instead we have people who never pull a penny out of their pockets, or almost never."

This story makes me think of the "passion" of the football team management in general. We're all losing money they say, and yet they want to be ever more involved, and yet none of them ever leave. Either this really is a great, great passion on their part…or, it is a very convenient passion.

Let's take President D'Attoma for example. Who ever heard of him? He was an industrialist like so many others. He talked about pants, and blue-jeans. Now he shoots out verdicts on the newspapers, does interviews, gets photographed, is highly publicized. And that's the point. There's no patronage or whoring like it. The Presidents have to pay a fee to enter the world of football. That is, the mechanism is turned upside down. Not that he puts in the money because he is good, or generous, or so we have to say thank you. No, he's the one that thanks others if anything, and he pays for the publicity like you pay to ride on a carousel.

Here we go again in Norcia. Castagner continues on his journey of distancing himself from us. He didn't know how to put together a human relationship that was worth having, but at least he was humble, shy, blushing from embarrassment even. Now his face doesn't turn red anymore. All those stories about the youngest manager in Italian football, about putting together a good team from potato peel players, about the Perugia collective, must have gone to his head.

It's as if there is another wall between him and us players, beyond the usual lack of communication. Last year I tried to understand something about him outside of football. Now I give up. I have the impression that if you take this man outside the stadium, away from the journalists, from the fans, he turns into an empty marionette. They say he votes Socialist, but every time he opens his mouth, out come man-in-the-street banalities: the delinquents, the thieves, the kidnappings? "You have to kill them all." That's his analysis. The kind of solutions you get from the silent majority, and really kind of stupid.

But this man has also become "serious." He doesn't mess around with us anymore, or screw something up and then laugh at himself. It seems like he has taken on in its entirety the role of the important person, someone who counts, who can't mix it up with his players.

A big disappointment.

Anyway, the narrative of the good manager and the weak team of Perugia came back to haunt them at the transfer window. After a winning season and one where we played well, no other organization asked for any of us. "All together they are good, but each one on their own?" So Perugia didn't get rid of anyone.

How is it possible, I ask myself, that coaches and journalists are so myopic? How can you say that a team is "made" by the manager? The team, always, for better is worse, is made by the players. What does it matter if Perugia doesn't have "names"? I know for certain that some of my teammates – Malizia, Nappi, Frosio, Curi, Scarpa, Vannini, Sabatini – are absolutely good. But you never hear anything said about them. You understand, there was Ilario with his magic wand. Sure, but if he launched us, we launched him. And much higher than before.

The bench, for Castagner, is the throne, his place in the sun. Who can take him down from it now? The journalists anoint him with incense, the fans idolize him, the team administration worship him.

That leaves the players. That half of the players hate him, with a genuine and true hatred that has nothing to do with jealousy, or with being excluded from the regular team, apparently is a fact of no importance.

Or maybe no one knows?

Who everyone does know about, and who should go to hell is Chinaglia together with his story about America. And to think he was even nice once. But the boos that they embroidered him with must have grated to pieces what little brain he still had, if in America he found the country of wonderland. It is certainly the right place for a foot-bollocks-er like him, right footed, and right-headed too. They even made up a joke about him. "What's the team with the biggest dick?" Lazio, because it has its dickhead in New Jersey, and its bollocks in Italy."

Gisella is a curse, she pops up in my thoughts like a car that jumps the guardrail and ends up in the opposite lane. An accident is inevitable, wounds, bites, and kisses, red ants all over you, cruel and pitiless. She slides around my sweat-filled eyes.

We train and I ask Walter if she is thinking of me. He's all twisted in some exercise on the limits of passing out. I sense his "fuck you" more than I hear it. I ask Zumbo while he is doing gymnastics on the floor, the "boat," a sort of seesaw you do on your stomach. He insults me too. I try Michele after a forty-meter dash, "go fuck yourselves, you and her."

In the end, I don't think she thinks about me much, in fact not at all. But thinking about whether she thinks about me helps pass the time.

Then there's Grazia who's with a man. I ask her how it's going. "With him everything is fine, we've been together for a short time, we talk a lot." Politically she says she has become more or less an anarchist. Or an artistic way of covering up not understanding anything. But it's already a step in the right direction.

Walter and Flavia are happy too. They've invented the "flirt," pronounced the way it's spelled, "fleert," nationalized, without English-isms. A "flirt" is less emotional than an "affair," more honest than a "loving friendship," less complicated than a "summer romance." Flavia has just one defect, especially for us footballers: she comes to the retreats. A year ago she went around with Paolo and now he plays in Serie D.

But in the end they all have us being demoted. In these prognostications, they don't know we have a secret weapon. And we spy on it all the time, we pass around news of it, we check in on it. It is a strange weapon, lethal, like an atomic umbrella. You can check on it in the cards: it's called Castagner's butt. Luck.

Basically, when he plays the first matches, there is some cause to worry, he loses, ties, rarely wins. A bad sign we think. Then he tucks in his buttocks and fortune comes our way again, mean, impetuous. This year too, we will be fine.

"You are against the football system," they tell me, "but what do you propose instead? How would you build the circus tent? How would you run the football clubs?"

Certainly, there is no magic that can solve everything all at once. But we can clear some paths. First of all, enough of the benefactor Presidents that make, undo and wreck things as they please. The structure of an football club can't depend on the moods and loves of some rich guy. The transformation into shareholding companies was an important step, and as head of these organizations there should be an administrator, not just some billionaire.

A salaried administrator who receives a specific mandate to do things, and is accountable to an administrative board. On this board, there should be, besides the usual shareholders, representatives of the fans, and of some local agencies. As a first step. Further on, the football club can even become part of the city council budget, as happened with the established theatres (but hopefully working out a little better). Heading up these clubs a municipal functionary, and the players become employees of the local agencies, solving the problem of "afterward." They'll find a job adapted to their abilities among the activities of the local associations.

This would allow us to reduce the absurdly high salaries of the professional football players, providing in exchange a livelihood and a place in the community. This would also enable the sport to avoid becoming a training ground for ignorance and individualism, an island unto itself, a forge turning out social and political outcasts.

It's clear that these changes won't come about by themselves, but will follow on the heels of a transformation of society. If this transformation happens, and I believe it will, even professional sports will have to adapt themselves to it. Otherwise, there's nothing to say. But if a change in political direction plows a deep furrow through the nation, knocking down the privileged classes in favor of the exploited, a solution will no longer be suspended in air.

Of course, we footballers have to do some work as well. I ask myself what category of workers can "boast" of having a union that is more leftist, more engaged in struggles, and more regularly attacked by the mass of its own members. And yet in football this is the case.

The Footballers Association is still seen as something extraneous, which might defend you in an economic controversy, but has no alternative meaning. And so, missing is that pressure from the base, without which the Association risks becoming a beast of burden and nothing else. On the other hand, the more politicized footballers prefer to act and be involved outside of football, and the rest get moving only if you step on their toes.

This is how we can explain a trade union that is only footballers-oriented, and only corporative. Struggles and initiatives get resolved only within the world of football, and you don't think about going outside on pain of death. A self-respecting union has to be connected to the rest of the labour movement, it has to deal with problems that don't only affect its own sector, it has to present goals that are somewhat more general in nature.

So why not make contact with the federation CGIL-CISL-UIL? Why stay away from the struggles over reforms, jobs, the cost of living, investments? Why not get involved in formulating a plan for sports that includes the building of athletic venues, the creation of sports centres, the development of instructors, all so as to met towards that famous idea of mass sports?

It's easy to see why: the Footballers Association is still a very ambiguous organization. It's a "colorless" trade union, a pastiche of all political ideas. It treats the interests of comrades and those of the more or less self-declared fascists, like Wilson and Petrelli in the same way. And this is possible because the players don't feel the need for a union that is more politically alive and mature, more advanced, closer to the rest of society; instead they actually tend to maintain it as a thing apart, privileged and uncontaminated. In this sense, the Footballers Association is the faithful mirror of the average footballer. It defends his narrow corporative interests, and has an I don't-give-a-damn attitude to all the rest.

Campana and Pasqualin would probably like to involve the union in external issues. But the union has to also respect its mandates, and I'm afraid that on certain issues that are even just a bit more political the only mandate it would get would be to go to hell.

Footballers too get sent there when they are no longer useful: Miguel Vitulano, Paolo Petraz, and Claudio Tinaglia are all ending up at Salernitana, definitively. From Serie A to Serie C, by way of the thirty matches that Claudio played there last year. If I were in his shoes, I wouldn't have gone. Of Miguel, I remember "go cry in Church," an Argentine saying that means don't complain, keep going, as soft or as hard a person as you may be. Walter too, sent to Varese to take care of his ankle. As soon as I make a football friend, they send him away. But it's the logical consequence of the flirt...

Walter tells me about D'Attoma's conversation with him. "Listen, I would have sent Sollier instead of y'all, but I wasn't able to ...." Naturally we laugh about this.

Naturally I will laugh the next time White Pen tells me, "Let's look each other in the eyes." This phrase is his pirate flag, the hook he hopes to use to catch you with, the swindle. You talk about money, about rewards, about deadlines. But you don't get out of the negotiations without that brand slogan. "My friend, let's look each other in the eyes," and you believe who knows what, if he says that it must mean it will be a frank talk. Then you realize that that phrase is a form of effortless hypnotism that allows him to stick it to you. Just like his kindness, because he is kind. But it's a tool to swindle you with. And so you do look him in the eyes, but as you would a snake that wants to bite you; and yet you do so laughing. By now, the phrase has become a kind of joke.

Like "doit" has. He is a lawyer that is expert in bricks, but a bit less in the Italian language. One day he is talking about a prize-match, and out comes "You all doit the result, and I will take care of paying for it."

And so "doit" has lasted.

Nicknames are a tribute every team demands. I answer to "Mao" after having been "Ho Chi Minh." Then there's Raffaeli with "Zumbo," for his African-like features and his cannibal tendencies. Nappi is called "Abebe," the prophet of cycling and running, or else "Chicken breast." Curi is called Gert by Muller, because in training he identifies with him. Vannini is "The Condor" for his camel-like gait, and for how high he jumps for headers. Frosio is "Milord," neat and proper like an Englishman. Amenta is "Mullet." Marchei is "Roundy" – for his tendency to get fat and so to roll around. Scarpa is "Bunny," for his rabbit-like fear, since to get him to enter the penalty area you have to sow it with carrots. Novellino is "Monzon," because he looks like him, and because he gets into fist-fights with everyone.

Gisella disappeared. Her scratches are more infectious than ever. I know it's stupid, but one can't make love from a distance, these kind of psychological bridges can only end up falling down, but now I am fixated on her lips. They walk all over my skin, they touch me, I bite them. They remind me of the last leaf on a tree that moves with every touch of the wind. They tremble. As if they had something cold inside, nervous. Then the leaf falls and it becomes a whole path of fallen leaves, every hue of brown. Her lips are like that, moist underneath, and dry above. And who knows how they become, how they get wet, how they open as the night becomes humid. They are full of wounds, of cutting cuts, of autumn. They are paths. It's just that in between the leaves there are also hedgehogs, and so it's dangerous to sit down.

You trampled on the flowerbed, yet another accusation. You use bad words, you stain the stadium with politics, the sport is pure, and various other crap along the same lines. Now, I do think that everything is political, from buying groceries to sitting on the loo, from getting a coffee to looking each other in the eyes. How can something that involves millions of people not be political? Something that fills up newspapers, that leads us to joy, hatred, drunkenness? Over which entire cities convulse, dress up in costumes, explode. Something that often works like a drug, as an excuse for forgetting, as a safety valve. Bartali winning the Tour de France at the same moment as the attempt on Togliatti is already a historical fact, with the anger at the gunshot and the desire to revolt compensated for by "national joy" of the sports victory.

And today, even if people are more mature, and are beginning to understand this ill-fated path, even today, this mechanism still works.

Toni, an ancient friend, a union delegate for workers at Stura, said during the last World Cup in Germany, "If by chance Italy wins, we won't be able to get anything done in the factory for three months."

He had the pulse of a situation already exposed by the swindles of fandom. Naturally, given the rarity of successes for Italians around the world, this danger of national hypnosis is somewhat reduced...

The substance of the argument stands. Namely, that sport practiced and rooted for, involves an enormous number of people, involves interests, leads to people spending and making money, leads to constructing stadiums, printing four daily sports newspapers, filling up the hours, televisions and bars. And so whoever keeps insisting that sports are apolitical, behind a pure agonistic barrier, in a neutral territory, is either an imbecile, or else they have already figured this stuff out for a while now, and they find this argument useful.

There's no such thing as the apolitical. Because whoever doesn't engage in politics, whoever doesn't get involved, whoever is uninterested, leaves it to others to do. Therefore they support those in power.

It's as if two people are fighting, and you are standing there watching, relaxed, apolitical, inhuman, being an asshole, rather than getting involved on behalf of the weaker one. In reality, by standing still you helped the stronger one, you let him use his power, you let him massacre the other one, all in the name of a false, cowardly, hypocritical neutrality. The same is true of political struggles: being neutral is an alibi no more credible in this case either. If you don't take a position, in reality you are complicit with the stronger side, ally of the constituted power.

Not by chance those who continue to sustain the apoliticalism of sports are either Christian Democrats or else declared reactionaries. To them it's fine if the fan shuts their eyes to what happens to other people. If you open them, who knows, you might end up getting your ass kicked.

As for me, the accusation is that I opportunistically use sports to do politics. Except that I do politics completely independent of the fact that I'm a footballer. And in my doing politics there is an argument to make in sports, a critical and alternative argument, an argument that says "no" to the using the stadium as the basin in which to wash away all of your frustrations, that pulls the knickers off the myth of the championship, that changes the relationship between players and fans. Everything clear, without camouflaging the matches with rallies.

And I ask: if sports are not political, why do they get used politically, confining them to an opportunistic neutral territory? If sports are not political, why is the fan functional to the system? If sports aren't political, what has always been the point of the priests making the children attend mass? If sports aren't political, why have their operation always faithfully reflected the political choices of the system we live in?

The answer is easy: it's all smoke, rooting, and rhetoric in our eyes. Imbecile or Christian Democrat, no one can fail to realize this reality.

Of course to be able to make an argument that makes this clear requires that the sports press have a different mission. Of the four daily sports papers, only *Tuttosport* has made this important choice. In fact there you find sports treated as news, critical commentary, etc. but above all you find sports with its social and political connections. There every day you find the basic political argument that ties the sporting event to reality, it reminds you of what is going on, it prevents the chloroformization of sports as an alibi. You find there a sports newspaper that is made to open up your eyes, a newspaper that is interesting and alive.

Of course, it's only a first try, a somewhat thwarted attempt to provide an example to the behavior of the rest of the press. The political newspapers generally treat sports with demeaning superficiality. There is the ever-present parochial journalism, the *campanilistic* exaltation of their team, of their athlete, of the player for Turin for *La Stampa*, for Rome for *Il Messaggero*; there is the fear of empty journalistic space, and the attempt to fill it; the investigations into sensationalism at all costs, scandals, provincialism, gossip. Three pages for the football derby, and two lines for Bayi setting a world record. Absurd.

Furthermore, these diseducational newspapers are the first to scream, astonished, when violence appears at the stadium, when something goes wrong, when periodically they realize that Italians are actually players that are sitting down.

It is just this manner of treating sports that feeds the mentality of being only a fan, that puts one to sleep instead of encouraging one to practice, that identifies people with whoever is the current champion. And so it doesn't matter much if the kids have curved spines, and the adults wear slippers all day and everyone's health is from over-the-counter-well-being. It doesn't matter much, after all, the champion wins for us. We are all Riva, Mazzola and Rivera. We are Moser and Mennea. They run, we watch, and they keep us content. The actual practice of sports is only for champions. And sweat is always, and only, something that stinks.

Sassi told me Novellino is good. Now I see him play with my own eyes. He's playing my position even now that I've healed up. Rightly so. I have to get my step, my running speed, my strength back again. He takes as many steps as he wants, he kicks the ball as if he were using his hands, he runs circles around the opponent. His nutmeg at Re Cecconi, got the whole stadium laughing. He is making every defender in Italy admonish themselves for not being able to stop him without physically beating him. It's quite a show. And I am now the reserve on the bench.

Enzo D'Orsi takes advantage of the situation to avenge himself: after the millionth time I attributed the nickname "*Novelleaduemila*" to him, he now replies with "*Novellinosettantasei*," and he lands a direct hit on me.

There are sad days, bad days, and boring days. And then there are the days that are just bent out of shape. Maybe I just needed to spend some more time in bed and everything would straighten out. Instead, I got up with my head spinning out of control; then came the match with Velez and heavy feet, and boos. Those at least were straight. Then a toothache. A twisted pain: one minute a *pickaxeing* gives you the illusion that it has passed; then the rock hits you in the head. I realize that I am staggering, grimacing with pain. If you were being tortured, then you suffer through the pain, and at least you would know you saved someone; if it were your lungs, feeling pins and needles from the cold, and you can't feel your hands anymore, at least you're in the mountains; if you were getting it up the ass from a friend, at least you are draining their sexual tension. But useless pain that you just have to endure to no useful end only makes me angry.

Like the flight of the vultures on Pier Paolo Pasolini. Around those that know everything, I feel kind of ignorant not knowing anything. I've only seen one of his movies, *Porcile*, and I liked it. I read some of his poetry. That famous one on the police being the children of proletarians, the ancestor of the police union, is beautiful but it's false. Nobody's ever had a problem with the individual cop, who probably had to choose between wearing the uniform and going hungry, but with the police who defend power with batons and teargas in the face.

That poem depicts the students as "daddy's children," without ever asking itself what these students really are, what their 1968 really is, how they unhinged the bourgeois dogmas; and yet on the other hand it humanizes the police as the individual cops, without ever asking what they are as a whole.

I haven't read his books; just some articles that someone told me about. But his provocations, the intuition he put into them, I like those.

Anyway, he got crushed under a car, and is now made fun of. Like a painter, after his death, his paintings and drawings, his words or scribbling, multiply in value. There's a seller, a buyer, and a middleman. In short, he got it up the ass, and not in the way he liked either.

It pisses me off when comrades become fans. I expect a different level of maturity from them; a behavior consistent with their ideas. What the hell? They have figured out how the world works, but they're still tangled up in calling the referee a cuckold, or throwing stones at the bus carrying the opposing team. As if going to the stadium was taking a vacation from their own ideas, from being consistent. The old game of the weekly break works on them too, the game of there being space where everything is allowed, permitted, accepted, and justified.

If being a comrade means living in a different way, if the personal is political and the political is personal, then I don't understand those comrades who are maybe great at activism, and who then transform themselves when they go to a match. They think they are acting as comrades by politicizing football slogans, or by calling the referee a fascist, or by trashing the grandstand. But it's a stupid alibi, they get corrupted by rooting like everyone else, and they end up drowning from it. I am not saying to not go to the stadium, on the contrary; but to go while remaining capable of judging, not taking sides at all costs.

The cheerful fan, rhythmed-up from the drumming, the cheers of people that meet each other on the *curva*, the songs, these are fun things, folkloric, and they put you in a good mood. But when this cheering turns violent, poisonous, a blunt instrument, then there's no excuse. And it's that much worse if those who do it are comrades.

Whenever I see one with their eyes dilated, sweating, with their throat paved with insults, excited, my balls drop. Where are we going with these people I ask myself, how mature are they? What different way of living? All they have to do is organize a Party and they are in there up to your throat. Fodder for flags, the little beaks of twenty-two birds hopping onto the field.

Her thinking of killing herself feels like a knife in my veins. I am certainly not the nail that can keep her fastened to her bad days; but I feel like I count for less than nothing. Other than going to bed together, other than our life on a double bed. There is only a single mattress: in the middle is her mouth, fountain and swamp, the nest of red ants, red lumps of my blood, pungent and useless.

Some comrades from San Benedetto come to see me on retreat. They tell me about a rugby team "Red Star," all made up of comrades, and about a fascist team they were supposed to play against. They refused to play the match and they were expelled from the Federation.

I don't really agree with their position, because it is only a way of getting ourselves ousted; as long as there are some spaces, we have to cover them, not leave them. Take it to the other team, prevent them in any case from becoming points of reference.

Instead now the comrades' team can't play anymore and that open sewer instead can. And they knew this before they even had to play them; what's the point of signing up for a competition and then essentially withdrawing from it? The political impact of the "example"? It doesn't seem sufficient to me, if we want to seriously confront the problem of sports, if we want to create alternative sports associations, ones that are really different, and run by comrades.

Seen in San Benedetto, "whoever reads this is a Christian Democrat."

Also in San Benedetto a comrade thrown in gaol for having torn down an MSI bulletin board with a circular saw. Protected by the Constitution?

I am beginning to doubt that this house will really become a commune, an open place, a reference point.

The relationship between Nico, Rossella and I feels like it's been bastardized; we don't have any practical problems, we don't argue, we even love each other; be we are not reciprocally involved with each other. Rather than being a new experience, we are an old-age pension.

And yet I have no doubts that this is the right way for me to live. The difficulty is finding other people who have more or less the same desire, who have the same mental crosses to bear, the encounters, the conflicts, and the things that have been lacking in previous situations.

With them it isn't like that, they are calmer, more programmed, less likely to be disturbed. They prefer to stay secluded. You see this really well when some comrade comes to visit. There's a chill, distance, etc. basically there's the difference between the homeowner and the visitor. In an alternative house this isn't supposed to happen, this gate-keeping is supposed to be dismantled, left aside.

But more than anything else the question becomes what road to take: while I tend as much as possible toward socialising, toward everything for everyone, they tend toward family-isation; toward a small circle of friends and that's all; towards a limited number of relationships with the outside world.

This means that even though we don't have any arguments, we can't live together, we can only occupy the same house; without ever risking any of our existential territory, our choices, our crises.

Take Nico. He's diffident, closed, cold. But also available, lively, ready to tear himself in two to do you a favour. You simply have to get to know him, get past his defenses with some Trojan Horse. As for the diffidence, with that face of an Arab that has lost his camel, he must have gone through a lot. And it shows.

Undoing this diffidence is hard. But I have discovered that he's the fastest coffee pot washer in Islam (it's not cold yet and he's already cleaned it even if someone else will just dirty it again), and that at night someone is cutting the tires on our cars, and that if we catch them we will vulcanize their assholes, and knowing all this you can drink a lot of coffee and then go help him find his camel.

Maybe we won't find anything, but that's the point: try. I used to think that before hanging out with someone you needed to know everything about them, to check out their ideological positions, count their emotional fleas, in short, be on the safe side. Instead, after all of these meticulous "investigations," my first experience was a total fiasco.

Four men and a woman, we ended up in a domestic guerilla war, everyone's door closed and us not even talking. The first "solution" was a purge, but Dario didn't want to leave. We decided to force him to. The form of struggle chosen to accomplish this was to cut off his sleep, hold his eyes open, not let him fall asleep. All night in his room singing, playing music, playing games, preparing food, anything to keep him awake and to force him to give up.

A dirty thing to do, mean, vile, certainly not comradely. But what did being comrades mean at that point, in that house? It was full of rancor, and tension; we wrote pamphlets against one another. We got carried away. Dario gave in.

After a month, Franco said "I'm leaving. I'm getting married tomorrow. Ciao." Around the same time Cinzia disappeared. But she at least had the excuse of her mother committing suicide. They found her dead in her home after two months. The flies were already dead too.

Gigi and I looking ourselves in the face. Overwhelmed, having fully survived on an island of astonishment, of disappointment, of defeat.

Since that time I don't make plans. What happens happens.

They talk about Monday. The day that the footballer husbands surrender themselves corporally to their spouses. And the bachelors go looking for sex.

To me it's infantilizing. Sunday evening is for sleeping late and "Mogadon" for being able to. The following Monday morning is fogbound; I keep drinking coffee to wake myself up. The whole day I wait for hands that will untie my brain, I desire only quiet, and then I get bored of the quiet, and then I get dissatisfied, I need to do something, ideas remain hidden, another coffee, a run around the course, four of us shooting the shit on the stairs in the piazza, a phone call with Walter, about the manager that likes him but doesn't put him in to play.

Monday there's also the mountain, Mount Subasio, but more than anything it is sub-ass. You walk so as to arrive absolutely nowhere, without ever reaching the top. I seek alms in the form of photos, but the snow is always dirtied with grass and stones, sickly. To find a drop of ice, or an unusual reflection is a task for a watchmaker. I feel my feet which I can't feel anymore.

Monday goes on. It always goes on. I'm free, and sockless, and foolish and shoed. Evening arrives and I wake up. Monday leaves me content. It's all pell-mell, confused and without any schedule. A day of doing fuck all, a day of vacation.

One in the morning, Claudia springs her trap: "Take me home." Bottoms up with words. I sometimes write things instead of doing them. She says them. Her Heaven must be two infinitely big, eternal ears that never tire of listening. It must infiltrate us with her voice, her crises, her counting her cravings on her fingers, basing it all on the sacred fire of theory. Or lamenting not having been in some place; she's never been there and wants to go there. Masculine places then.

"I want to kiss so many people; not to make love, just to taste their lips, to touch them. Women too, then I don't do it. The idea makes me tremble, maybe doing it would make it stop. Understand?"

I understand. Saint Repression pray for us. If you want to put your mouth to someone, then do it, that's all. Without asking yourself what you believe in, what you were thinking, what is happening. It's her problem. If you say ciao to someone, you don't ask yourself if they are going to reply or not, or tell them to die, or wonder if they didn't hear you, or fall apart. And this should be like saying ciao: get rid of the idea that kissing someone is like some phone call to the Netherlands that you have to get yourself ready for.

Grazia asked me why we don't stay together. Yeah. There aren't any ideological barriers anymore, her fascisms are a memory, she moved left on her own steam. She's changed. She's no longer a fascist, she's no longer a curse, and she's no longer distant. Consequently, it doesn't work for me anymore. The simplicity of my nonsense is amazing.

I'm starting to think that falling in love is just a way to make friends.

If they ever create a chair of assorted violence, specialist in athletics, I feel like I couldn't miss getting the job. They make me talk about it every day. It's the times, I understand. But this assault on violence, on its motivations, which repeats every year, shows how sterile it is to talk about it, and how there are no solutions, at least not any that are not long-term.

We live in an unjust society that every day teaches us violence, dominance and abuse. Where the strong, the rich, the to-the-manor-born, are untouchable. Where everyone feels isolated, impotent, unable to change. Work that doesn't mean anything, that doesn't interest you, flat, repetitive, *fancyplain*; cities that every day look more like dormitory chicken coops, where you rest so that you can produce more the next day; families in crisis, little nests of affection unable to open themselves up, closed in on themselves, suffocating; and how we ourselves are all buried beneath our resignation, all of our enthusiasm cast before swine, before fear. How many think they live badly, and that it isn't worth it. For how many is soldiering on just a form of atrocious collective suicide.

At this point either there is awareness, or you let yourself go. To take awareness by the throat and assault it, becoming violent, moving, acting. To take aim at the problems, finding others that have them too, talking about them, engaging in struggle. Kicking the structures of this system in the ass, dismantling this crushing system requires intellectual codfish and emotional herrings. We have to become goldfish instead, but ferocious ones. Swimming in the shit, but purifying it as we go. With kicks and spits. Arguing with the world, so as to make a better one.

Or else let yourself go with the flow. And the flow carries you to the stadium, to mass ejaculation, to fandom. It can all be good, and end in having fun, shouts and applause. And it can all go bad, all that anger that gets jammed up and doesn't find the right safety valve, all that dissatisfaction that finds yet more dissatisfaction. And so there's violence. Berlinguer had a nice turn of phrase when he said that the stadium is no longer a drug, that the mechanism of rooting as a way to blow off steam had been broken. I don't know if he goes to see matches, or if this is another part of the historic bullshit, but in any case it's not true. I have seen every part of the stadiums – field, grandstand, the *curva*, the straights – and rooting as a social illness is far from overcome. Because if on the one hand people mature, on the other hand the contradictions, and their frustrations, grow. The facts of this year demonstrate this, demonstrate the air of tension in the stadium, the air of war that you breathe in.

Anyone who is not politicized, and who undergoes all week long the torture of working, of high prices, of counting for nothing, becomes a potential human bomb. The press has armed him, he's armed himself by discussing things, by betting on things, by selling his ass to the betting form, by paying through the teeth for the tickets to the match. Then, if his team loses the match, and plays poorly, or the referee invents some things, the fan becomes violent and dangerous.

Due to political immaturity, and because he's not athletic. And he's not athletic because he's never played sports. And he's never played because they never let him, because they never built the structures for that, because he's not a champion. Because mass sports activity doesn't exist. Let's take a good look at ourselves within: children have to play in between the cars, have to run on asphalt, and to swim they have to go and drown in the canals. And let's not even mention the adults. Those few who have the desire have to go running alongside cars on the roadside, breathing in exhaust and risking their lives.

In short, practicing sports, sweating because afterward you feel better, the satisfaction of breathing deeply, are yet again things for the rich.

School, someone says… certainly school is the right place, or rather it should be. Everything starts from there. But we have to make up for years in which the hour for gymnastics was needed for study, or was wasted in discipline training, with teachers and programs suffering from physical and mental paralysis.

Today those who went through this see sports as something for others to wear, or, if they put it on every now and then, it's as folklore, as an event, as a party costume. So look at long-distance running, sprinting, running in circles, all positive, nice facts, but done as substitutes, as an alibi, as a used band-aid. You want to know why they are still considered strange things, that add color to life, that are surprising, unmoored from everyday life, because they provide release from the question of sports structures, of organization, of sport as social service. Why spend money, someone might ask, when these people run alongside the road and seem happy?

And so we keep on with our putting up with things, or going to the parish; we settle for whatever, and smuggle in sports when possible. So, in the end, the only real mass "sport" is being a fan, and the people keep finding themselves using the only part of the stadium that is allowed to them, namely the grandstand. With what results we know.

There are no immediate solutions. The repression, police tear-gas, the wolf-dogs, won't work. The security forces of organized fandom can only block the actions of the isolated kamikaze, the provocateurs, they can kick the ass of the fascist thugs, or the dubious little leftist groups that want to start a riot; they certainly don't solve the root problem, precisely because this root sucks deeply into our society, and to deal with it you need to change society.

But we can start by removing what we might call the benign tumors, like the parochial journalism, the victimism of the players, and how we use slow-motion in the case of referees (show when they get it right, rather than only when they make a mistake).

Violence in the stadium walks hand in hand with violence in society at large. They are relatives. One leads to the other. And so long as this society isn't transformed, troubles at the stadiums will be one of its many mirrors. Beyond which, this particular mirror includes the sports press and the dribbling-stuntmen falling down on the field.

Many sports journalists protest their innocence, not responsible in any way, *PontiusPilates* who wash their pens of the problem. Then they spend the whole week embroidering Bettega's underwear, counting the fleas on Rivera, running behind the airplane voyages of Chinaglia. Not to mention the orgy of Mondays in the political newspapers: all the chronicles, the results, the doubts, the penalties, the rants, half the entire newspaper devoted to the football season, to the divas; in the other half, almost smuggled in, as if to excuse ourselves for putting it there, the political, social, cultural news of the day. As if they were afraid of "disturbing" the reader, of distracting them from the sports chronicles. It makes you want to vomit, and in the vomit you'll find even newspapers like *L'Unità* that say that they want to create a different sports politics. You can see that on Monday at least, it's more important to them to sell newspapers.

Victimism, somersaultism, chiarugismo, the double and triple heads-over-heels on every impact, the complaints and the theatre, staying on the ground as if you've been boned like a fish, and two minutes later tripping people like before, happy to have taken the piss out of everyone.

If I were a referee I'd come down hard with red cards. These mother-loving scenes of holding the tibia or the fibula are ways of whipping up, injecting excitement directly into an already warmed-up crowd; they're dangerous and should be punished. If someone stays down on the ground, put them on a stretcher, otherwise they should get up. There's no such thing as miracles and magic sponges. Only spoiled marionettes; cut their strings, and don't give them another thought.

What a disaster with Roberta. It's impossible to have any exchange, knot, bruise, caress. Everything's impossible. Except smoking. Her mental *streamofconsciousness* is unbearable, like hallucinating. Her lines – political, emotional, even the lines of her hands – are twisted and embarrassing, each one contradicting the others. You don't know if she says this shit because she's smoked too much, or if she actually thinks this stuff and the smoke melts her boundaries.

These hippies, I understand why they're covered in flowers. They're dead.

We smoked. It was the first time. The last barrier of diffidence and of FIFA was pierced by the Monday magic. I relaxed and took a hit.

For a non-smoker it went well: only two hundred coughs and a few kilometers of my throat without its tree bark. I felt a breath in my brain, suddenly everything was frosty and sparkling. Like lying down in below zero temperature with a pleasing feeling of warmth. Like falling backward into chairs that are increasingly soft, comfortable, snowy, hot.

Then we changed fuels and I was ill. My eyes danced, everything jumped from one pupil to another, as if my brain had shrunk and danced around in its box. Pain all over, heavy bleeding, fear of falling out of my body, my pupils looking like Flipper's…

I'll probably smoke again, but I was unconvinced and I remain unconvinced.

War in Perugia, the New Years Eve Rebellion. Everyone on retreat says Castagner, to avoid temptation and limitless blowjobs. In fact, in his opinion, players wait for 31 December to fuck and to stay out all night. Before then no. Nor after. Just that night.

Fabrizio, Berni, Michele, Nappi and I decide to refuse to go on retreat; for different reasons, clearly. They so as to spend New Years Eve however they want, I so as to not to spend it. It's been years since I celebrated it, so that I would have even forgotten that it exists, if it weren't for other people's shit. Not to be contrarian at all costs, but because these holiday expiration dates no longer mean anything. What does it begin and what does it bring to an end? Nothing. It's an artificial dam put there to uncork bottles and pretend to enjoy yourself.

The last New Years Eve that I "celebrated" was back in the days of being in "Outstretched Hands," when we went around to houses collecting paper and rags for our farm in Chubut. These dressed up and necklaced people opened their doors to us, and we asked them if they had any old newspapers, magazines, and old clothes. An incredible contrast. We collected very little stuff and a lot of go fuck yourselves.

And so now I should go on retreat to avoid "occasions for temptation"?

Castagner loses his temper. "There are a lot of senior executives that are already angry with you for that whole affair about the uniform. You want to get them even angrier?"

Yeah, the uniform. The big find of the year. We're a serious team, so we have to all dress the same. Like good little children, all queued up in a row. I don't know if this mentality is born of affective imbalances or from militaristic manias, or just from stupidity. Whatever the cause, my teammates now go around in a jacket the color of drunken vomit, like the Casadei Orchestra. Naturally, I refused. Mainly because I hate uniforms, and also because I want to dress as I please, and not as some fashion maniac has dreamed up.

I had already thought of everything. I don't go and I send the money I would have spent to the Workers' Daily. A revolutionary use for a useless love. Instead I surrender *in extremis*. I make it to the airplane by a hair, racing, cursing. Then a Europe of clouds. Copenhagen. I rent a car, I ask in English and strangely they really give me the car, and I go looking for the blonde umbilical cord. She is, she has been, she once was.

A strange nothing with her. Her with her man, with her Christmas with her parents, I come to understand that it's late, I'm not sure what it's late for, but it's late. As if I had missed an I don't know what, a train, a snail, a caress. Something that doesn't come again and leaves behind a trail, a sound, a railroad track, a scar. Her always carved in the wood of her own charm. Her man who looks like Jesus Christ before the miracles. Me alone on a second hand sea, facing Sweden. Goddamn Denmark.

It doesn't work anymore. It's as if she had abandoned me after years of psychological living together, leaving me only old photos and cold Danish. The idea of not going was the right one.

Only the thought of Gisella to console me. A sort of changing of the guard.

A monument in a yard. A girl on a bicycle in the light of a lighthouse, in the rain. It moved me, I was that little girl running in the street, happy, pedalling right under a car, the bike twisted, the blood, the silence, the sound of the sea. The father and mother spend their last energy on that statue and then close themselves up in their house.

Ascoli, kick and run. Legnaro and I pedal shoulder to shoulder, elbowing, hands in the sides to pull yourself forward. The ball goes out. So do we. At that point he gives me a kick, the kind that could fracture something. It catches me. "Are you crazy?" I ask him. He replies "You play with your hands, so I teach you with my feet." But if I grab you by the shirt, I reply, it don't hurt you, but kicks do. "Go make speeches at campaign rallies" is his response.

Look at this imbecile, I think, now I'm going to give him campaign rallies. That moment sparks something, from then I play half for the ball, half just with my leg, my cleats at nose level. At the last minute a ball gets shot up in the air, and Novellino scores the winning goal. Successful campaign rally I shout, but I don't think anyone heard it, with their ears full of boos and Madonnas.

It's my first win in Serie A. Homage to that cretin who while I took a corner, shouted Viva Mussolini.

It's done. I'm a homosexual. Giuseppina Manin does an interview with me that is a bit more open, and so naturally I say that I have nothing against homosexuality. It's just that for now I don't feel the need – due to repression? – for relations with men.

Everyone starts asking me if I am an ass man. Or else they ask cautiously, "But were those things you said about sex true?." Yes, they were true, but leave me alone. This year, everything I touch ends up as a controversy. I transform the simplest things into ideological conflicts. Maybe it's deserved, maybe I went looking for it, but it's always me that ends up here retracing my steps, trying to identify which ones were mistaken, stumbling over them.

The crowning achievement is the attack in *Giornale Nuovo*. They say I elbow my way through to popularity with the trick of sneaking through tight squeezes. Truly Montanellian.

But returning to sex, this accusation (which is not offensive, let's be clear) has helped me to unravel my own behavior. From the first, I felt uncomfortable, on the defensive. Then I liberated myself of these repressive lice, and squishing them one by one I came to realize how many there were and how much harm they can do. How homosexuals are mistreated, marginalized, torn to pieces. How the system, and "good people" discriminate against them and lynch them. Isn't it worth noting that "sexual normality" doesn't exist? That the norm, namely the behavior of the many, can't in every case be a rule valid for everyone? That everyone should live their own sexuality as they believe best, without repressing or being repressed? That being "different" is a right? That sexism, sexual discrimination, is nothing but the last orgy of racism, since racism is considering others to be inferior, calibrated to eliminate those who wear a different sexual skin?

I certainly feel more homosexual than I do prettyboyimperialist, at least at the level of where I stand. It's just that male flesh doesn't attract me. The last and only opportunity I have had to go with a man was on a train to Paris, some years ago. I turned him down. When will the next time be?

Even now, when I think about it, when I ask myself, when I explore myself, this homosexuality slides out from inside me. Letting someone do it to me in the ass doesn't really scare me, but it doesn't attract me either. If I think of a man I like, of those that pass me on the street and I think how nice they seem, a Lanzi in other words, if I think of kissing him or giving him a blowjob (I think I would be very good at it) the tongue playing with mine immediately changes sex. It becomes Gisella's, or Maria's, or Golden Eyes', and the dick in my mouth becomes a pussy, the legs around my neck become feminine. A sort of instinctive detour that has nothing to do with repression or with a stone wall.

Gisella's tongue. Gisella's trouble.

The trouble is that I am madly in love. When she smiles all my false teeth fall out. The lightning rods and the lightning. Of course there's tension. Of course after an hour we tell each other to go to hell. "Do want to get in bed?" she fires at me treasonously. But yeah, of course, in bed.

Holy shit, we get inside each other, we sink at least a claw into each other's flesh, we howl into each other's mouth. But it's not enough. What would be enough for me she can't give me. And logically in bed more men get inside her than get in her head.

Now I even understand her invented word "rabbleman." It's the male as rabble, the crew member, the crowd, the gathering, the doorman, all those people that stand in front of me with all their crap. And I push, and push, and elbow my way but I am still always in the back.

A Lanzi in other words. The handsome Enrico has fortunately filled the void left by Walter. Put to the difficult test of rooming with Zumbo, he managed to survive, and so for that reason has been consigned to the band of "slow children."

He comes for dinner one evening. We talk about footballers – jumped-up and not. Of how Novellino for example, is not jumped-up because he's tasted the hard life, and it's not a taste you forget. And Henry: "What, you want to call yourself jumped-up because we are little shits here kicking a football? I remember when we used to wash ourselves in the canal, and every now and then a dead pig would float down. The first one would tell all the others that the pig was on its way. And we kept washing ourselves. Jumped-up? I saw them leaving with their lunch pails to go work at Breda. It's hard, you can be sure of that. I would send those pretty-boys that take walks in the center of town to…"

Or, how to make a political statement while also saying that you don't understand a thing about politics…

I've always wondered why people talk so much about football, aside from it being nice. In fact, it's just as nice to talk about a lot of other things. About yourselves, about your problems, about what you want, about resisting what you want, about politics, about which party or group you root for, what a great midfielder that Berlinguer, what a great batsman Almirante is, how good Tanassi is at dribbling trials.

Instead no, you only talk about football. Zac is always Zaccarelli, never Zaccagnini, and the bribes are only about joint ownership of the team, never about the Lockheed scandal.

Why? A first answer is identification. Seeing yourself reflected in Gigi Riva is undoubtedly more stimulating than to hunchback yourself in Andreotti. And if you have to choose a "lion," Vinicio would be better on the Presidential carpet.

Then there's probably the fact that talking passionately about football doesn't do any harm; it makes you mad but it doesn't endanger your serene life. It makes you happy or makes you unhappy, but it doesn't pose problems of identity or of life choices. It's like fighting a war in a neutral territory. You can allow yourself the deaths and massacres, the bombs and napalm; it's the skin off no one's nose.

And after all talking about football is easy. Everyone's an expert and everyone has their opinion. There is no mathematical solution, the ball is round, etc. Almost everyone has played it, from the old-time professional to the guy who had to play goalkeeper because he wasn't any good. Everyone knows how a kick to the ankle or an elbow in the side feels. To everyone it just seems like you take the field, run, dribble. There's almost a national identity in this sport that's played in the parishes, in the courtyards, alongside the streams, in the car parks, on the beaches. So talking about it then becomes kind of obligatory, a kind of phony bridge between people, given the inability to talk about yourself, to really communicate.

She calls me one night from Rome. "I'm coming but I'm not sleeping at your place." Why? "I can't say on the phone." But why? Are they listening in on you? Just speak in Piedmontese dialect ! "I can't…" One of the worst shitty phone calls from Meucci on down.

What does she want, sexual safety? She knows that as a sexual violator I am not worth much. Or maybe it's Toni's science fiction hypothesis: that she is menstruating, and that she is afraid of suffering too much from the desire to fuck me?

Or that she really is crazy and a slut, and she's keeping her distance so as feel closer? Or…

Or maybe Claudia has squished the right insect, namely, that she is going out with a man, some Piedmontese bastard, and it seems a little too much to her to come here and fuck me at home.

Too much is too much, but I will put up with it. I went to Denmark to see Bente twist herself around some German guy, I can put up with a regional intertwining. Certainly, the old hospitality will be hard.

Don't even dream of holding her hand; offer a handshake to that fucking Piedmontese. She's on the other side. I will touch her over his dead body.

Nothing doing. I am hurt, suffering, and I am trying to hide it as little as possible. I am not seeking revenge. It's like Mavi taroted: my character is sensibility and rationality, a fucking Capricorn, together, like red and white, inseparable, one helps the other. To be what, then?

An egg, beaten too long. And the chicken came first. *Ras le bol*.

The fans of Lazio have already done a lot of damage in Parugia. Beatings, bolt cutters, chains. But what they managed to do at the Lazio-Perugia match deserves a firing squad.

Maybe it's unfair to say "the fans of Lazio," it would be more precise to say "the Lazio fascists." They beat people up, attacked buses, cut tires.

The next day, in the newspapers, no sign at all of this. Mild disturbances, they said. And the people in the hospital? And that gang that with fifteen minutes to go till the end of the match, that entered the stadium prepared for war? And that bastard that went around with a wooden pole in his hands like a blender among the Perugian fans?

To not denounce these things is not only complicit. It invites it to continue, it licenses them to use violence. Of course it is much easier to blame me, it's more colorful, and it sells more newspapers.

All because of an interview. It came out in the *Messagero* Sunday morning. "If we win, we will have beaten Mussolini's team." Naturally, what I actually said was something else. "I know that Lazio has right wing tendencies, but when I play it could be the actual team of Mussolini and it wouldn't make any difference." A misunderstanding, nothing more. I don't doubt the good will of the journalist. But for those idiots of the *Nazione*, it's all my fault: "The fans don't want to risk getting beaten up for Sollier."

They don't mention that the Lazio ultras use violence every Sunday at the match. That for the whole week before we arrived they threatened us with attacks and blitzes. They don't mention that those bastards are fascists, they don't say that right up to

Saturday afternoon the whole FUAN of Rome was mobilized, they don't mention that you don't organize a banner like that at the last minute because of an interview in a newspaper.

Berni had warned me that some players on Lazio were "waiting for me." Instead, who was waiting for me were the ultras at the *curva*. Boos every time I had the ball, *Chinaglia-esquely*, then Castagner had the bright idea to substitute for me, and I leave with that banner "Sollier asshole!" right in front of my eyes, white on blue, five metres long. Sollier asshole chanted in unison by those shits, every hand on the *curva* shitted out in the fascist salute, me slipping into the underpass without a gesture. If I had raised my fist it would have just been mirroring their insults, a victory for them; so, not even a thread out of place. Inside: flayed alive, chewed up, scared. Shaking up to my ass, wishing I had a machine gun to shoot everyone on the *curva*, to make up for that stadium in Santiago.

And now anger for those *ratmouseturds* that defend them.

Naples-Perugia, a moment of silence for the earthquake in Friuli. The passage from fandom to complete silence is one long hiss: *ssst, quiet, ssst*, as if the stadium suddenly became an air chamber with holes in it, all the shouting deflated.

These minutes of silence make you think: in bursts, electrically, repeatedly; ideas come to you, revelations, weirdness, then come people, moments, stupidities. Too many things for sixty seconds. Only one thing is missing: you never think about the dead.

"Let'slookeachotherintheeyes" told me instead that I should never talk to journalists again, especially to those of Perugia, who, "we all know are not worth their ballpoint pens." I have to say in his honor that this time he acted correctly, defending me in the face of public opinion.

He added however that I have to stop putting myself on stage, because my teammates aren't happy about it, I'm getting all the attention.

I don't think that this is true, because mine is not a football notoriety, like those that enable you to get paid more next season, or that give you gratuitous credit that doesn't belong to you. This celebrity is born from, and lives on, the idea that a footballer can't be a communist militant. I don't think that another footballer can be jealous of this. And if one of them is, he only has to do as I do, come out into the open, make the relevant choices and refusals. This way, we can start a mass movement, and this kind of celebrity, and also the asshole footballers, will disappear.

All about Perugia: that it's beautiful and ugly, that it charms you and puts you to sleep; but when it rains, there's no place to go. The shiny roofs, the city wall that has endured centuries, the clouds that slip into the alleyways, clinging to the street corners, sifting through the water. The streets like mountain paths, with streams that flow into the middle of everything and strip the stones clean. The sounds that smash things to pieces, humid, drained, the smell of wet smoke. All that's missing is the polenta and every storm would become a party.

The danger is past. She arrives without a man. Nor alone. She doesn't come.

For the price of ten coins in the telephone slot she has taught me a complete course of excuseography.

"You know, I don't really feel well; and for just one day it's not worth it. And I don't know the train schedule…."

Not to be presumptuous, I tell her, but these are Pinocchioesque lies: short legs, long nose, little monsters, taking the piss. Let's tell it like it is.

Then, luckily, I ran out of coins. The last one brought her down too, and she brought me down, all night the law of the millstone around our necks. The level of shit rises, that of Gisella sinks, along with the famous law of communicating vessels. Chamber pots, a barricade, a wall, a guardrail of chamber pots, between her and I, between my bollocks and hers.

At the Perugia-Fiorentina match, some spectators forced the gates and entered without paying. They did the right thing. Not because it's right to enter gratis. But as a form of struggle and protest over the rising cost of living. The ticket prices are already high, I don't see why for the important matches they should cost even more. This is the black market, Sunday afternoon bullshit.

You can't spend five or six thousand liras on a football match. It's true that the lira isn't worth a lira anymore, but it's still too much.

The primary excuse for it by the football clubs is the players' salaries. They make too much, the administrative expenses are high, we aren't making ends meet. They never say of course that the deficit is due to the ridiculous purchasing campaigns, to the billions of lire peeled off all around, and let's throw the players' capital into the balance as well.

How can you consider a player as if they were a piece of land or a house? If Savoldi decides that he isn't going to play anymore, that he's not having fun anymore, if he takes a head butt that is much worse than usual, who covers the hole in the budget? Or what if a player valued at half a billion liras has a bad season, plays poorly, and gets resold for 300 millions, who puts in the other two-hundred millions?

The first way to get out of this mess will be the abolition of the famous reserve clause, and so even the cow market will disappear as well. And with them the stupid budgets that confuse numbers with meniscuses.

"You want to ruin everything" is the accusation made against the Players' Association. "Without the reserve clauses the tree nurseries disappear…Who will still have an interest in 'cultivating' players?"

What "ruin everything?" We just have to study the math, look at the tables. Study the tables, fix an age. Eighteen? Okay, until which the player will be under the reserve clause. Then, establish a reward for "cultivation" for the club, depending on whether the kid ends up in A, B, or C.

This solves the problem of the tree nurseries, so that whoever trains the players, whoever teaches them best, is in any case recompensed.

As for players changing teams, there are other tables to use. On age, appearances, salary, the position, and you calculate the sum that one team pays the other for the transfer. Sums naturally much inferior to those we see today.

This would allow us to get rid of another swollen lymph node on society, namely, off-the-books payments. Right now the clubs' wallets are emptied willingly on money outside of the contract so that they can avoid paying taxes and benefits, but later on these become self-inflicted wounds.

Who would give off-the-books money knowing that the value of the player also depended on their salary, and so if their salary is low, so will the amount be that he pockets. You would lose money twice, first off-the-books, then the non-money from the player transfer. No one would be so foolish.

But, those most opposed to abolishing the reserve clause, even more than the League and the clubs, are the players themselves. For a lot of them, things are fine the way they are. And for a lot of others, the dominant mentality is to change things as little as possible, for fear of the new.

The first goal in any case should be the signing off by the interested party on every transfer. It's absurd that a person can be sent from one city to another like a package sent by post.

"But you're professionals, you make a lot of money…" they say. It's an argument that doesn't hold up. There are a lot of professionals — lawyers, doctors, notaries, actors, singers — and they all get paid a lot. And yet they decide themselves where to live and work. That there are then others — workers, emigrants, unemployed — that don't make anything, is a problem that concerns us all, not only footballers. At least it concerns all those who make too much, whether they are bosses, merchants or journalists, including those journalists who libel the earnings of footballers.

Let's take the journalist Italo Cucci, right wing but pretending to be neutral, like all those who have always served power pretending to be moderates, balance scales, peacemakers. One move to the right, one to the left, so as to content the two opposed so-called extremes.

Naturally, I'm a target. They ask him what he thinks of that damned raised fist; and he replies that you don't bring politics into sports. But an intelligent reader puts him to the test: "Why are you criticizing Sollier for the raised fist and not with the various signs of the cross that the others make? Aren't they both expressions of a faith that maybe you don't share but we have to accept?" He replies that the fist is a violent gesture, while the sign of the cross "…is universally recognized as a symbol of peace."

It is difficult to find a better example of someone who lives in a glass house. He isn't just throwing stones, he's flying around in it. Maybe it's worth reminding him that a symbol stands for peace or for war or for love depending on the moment, and on the latitude, and on the century. The feminist symbol of hands forming a pussy stand for recognition, joy, peace among themselves, but war on sexism. The journalist Cucci certainly doesn't go to the Festa dell'*Unità*, or the festivals of the left, but he would do well to go to do so at least once, so he could learn that the raised fist is a symbol of equality, of feeling ourselves united, close to each other, friends.

As far as the sign of the cross is concerned, does signor Cucci remember how many people were massacred, tortured, shredded, precisely in the name of that symbol? Not to mention how often Sister Pagliuca did such things? And why doesn't he go to Lebanon or to Palestine or to Ireland to see if this symbol represents universal peace? Unless by peace he means the highly religious Franco and Pinochet, because that would explain everything.

It would also explain how in the world a magazine like *Guerino Sportivo*, which had the chance to be a great sports weekly, truly critical, visionary, alternative, remains instead a trash-talking magazine, a rumor-mongering scandal sheet.

Talis direttoris, talis redattoris. They even managed to present, in the appropriate section, "the Sollier football pool": admirable, not only because I never spoke to a single one of them, but also because I never play football pools. And the interviews? The journalists of the Guerino are so talented they manage to do them without even talking with the interviewees. It happened to me as well, "interviewed" for three full pages by a certain Claudio Sabattini that I have neither seen nor met.

Another javelin throw from "Cucci-Cucci-I-smell-a-Christianucci" is of course reserved for my earnings. "What's he doing making all these arguments, this guy that's so highly paid?" I would exchange my bank account for his in a minute, but I doubt that he would agree to it...In fact the highly paid Sollier doesn't exist. At least not until I voluntarily expropriate myself. Maybe signor Cucci and a lot of other people haven't figured out what it means to be a communist activist, or what it means to be different from them.

It means that whoever has money makes it available to the movement, to comrades, to our newspapers which are notoriously not financed by oil barons. It means giving millions not expecting it back, spreading it out, and one million leads to more. It means paying bills for others and amputating without mercy your own bank account. It means bankrolling comrades who have no money, and arguing with the residual bourgeois that tell you to "put something away."

In a certain sense it's also an investment. Making life different. My consciousness – first convinced Christian, now class conscious – has already enabled me to understand that since I don't own land or a house, it will make me dorm with others, it will love me, and it will stick a finger up my ass, and after that, plague and cuckolding.

Plague and cuckolding on me that I still manage to astonish myself; it's imbecilic. In this situation of being a divo, an anti-divo, a bollocksdivo, I have:

1. friends
2. comrades
3. admirers
4. those who don't give a damn but are nice
5. those who don't give a damn but are mean
6. those who are okay with me if I don't talk about politics
7. enemies
8. fascists

I can't change the minds of most of these, nor allow myself to be hurt by them. I can only concern myself with 1, 2 and 7.

The first because they make me live. The second to engage in struggle together. The seventh for comparison, contrast, and war. The others I don't have to listen to. I can't stand there screaming at the right, getting myself angry over having things like they were before. Or getting angry if someone writes that if I were a better footballer, I "would think less." These, more than low blows, are cheap shots.

Those journalists that suddenly "discover" that I don't know how to trap the ball, or that I'm slow-footed, make me laugh. I know, they have always known it. It's been some time that I have identified the qualitative crisis of the game of football as being not that I've gone up a category, but that football's gone down a level. What can I do about it? If they make me play, it's because I'm useful, to use the gifts I do have, not to put on display those I don't have.

A lot of journalists continue to confuse the smoke with the roast. If someone works a lot, it's clear that they will also make a lot of mistakes. You have to do the maths and see the results. The result this year speaks clearly: from the time Agroppi and I arrived, legs and heads, the team has been grinding. And grinding and grinding, it saved itself. If it had only made those three or four possible goals, it would have been a perfect season, but even so it is largely positive. So what does that Bertoldi mean when he says that Serie A is too much for my technical level? Who played the matches, him? What does technical level even mean? Hasn't he understood yet that on a team you need ponies and mules? That while I am certainly no pony, Novellino could never be a mule?

These journalists are also very presumptuous. Our play got them into Serie A, certainly not their professional abilities. And now they make enlightened criticisms... For sure if my play isn't at the level of a footballer in Serie A, theirs is that of third-rate journalists. Everything considered, I think it's better not to know how to trap the ball than to not know how to write or to write stupid stuff. I can always struggle, run, guess when a rebound will be; or, who knows, become a journalist. But them? All that remains to them is to change profession. Or go work for the *Nazione*. They'll take them, the discarded and the dysfunctional are always welcome there. It's part of the political line of the newspaper.

Another of these journalists is Marco degli Innocenti, first in line in Italy among the salary-stealers. He makes a ton of money every month for writing a thirty-line article, and not even one every day. Plus he acts like your friend so he can fuck you even further up the ass, convinced that he is acting like a great journalist, always in search of a scoop, an indiscretion, an exclusive.

During the match with Inter, he managed brilliantly in his imitation of a worm. We're in the press box; during the halftime, *Teleumbria* interviews us together. And he says, "A terrible match, Perugia is in trouble, it's clear they miss Sollier, I don't know why he was kept out." After an entire in week in which he had written that I wasn't in condition, I needed substituting, I should be eliminated, I should be thrown out.

This journalistass is always around the course, parroting someone on safari, clumsily, ridiculously, having suffered his Waterloo. Sweet girls are transformed into cruel Herods, doomed by the impossibility of putting up with him, and to perpetuate the Massacre of the Innocenti.

Golden Eyes is exceptional. If she entrances you with a look and a smile all at once, you're done for and finished. She's like an eclipse, a comet, a slice of light from a lighthouse that shipwrecks you, and makes you end up breaking your knee on the rocks. All it takes is that one time, and you're fractured for life. She makes your molecules fall in love. She makes you feel the anodes and cathodes, the ass and the dick, she makes you rage, makes you spit energy, recharges you. She's like a lightning bolt that explodes inside of her, illuminating her, and making me, old electrician that I am, ask myself what strange voltage makes her tick.

Entering inside her must be like sticking two fingers in the socket, like when you were a kid. And then the rest of your life you will be careful.

Rosanna got married. On the right or the left, for laughs or for real, for their kids or for their fathers, everyone gets married. They say they did it as a joke, decided on one cheerful evening. Good. It occurs to me that joking is a key to opening doors that being serious you are ashamed to even go near.

I remember when we went around to all the traffic jams, to unravel all the traffic we had going through our heads. Now I have the impression that she doesn't want any more traffic jams; she's searching for green lights and a straightaway.

Perugia and its university for foreigners: the biggest bluff ever. It's famous all over the world, and it's like a cultural lump that has nothing to do with the city.

Maybe at one time it really was a scalpel, a tool that dug, opened, rummaged. But now if you take out a few politicized Palestinian or Iranian students, bitten by their dead, the others are fauna for budgets, for local color, for safari.

They have no relationship with the flow of real life, with the numbness and the sudden reawakenings of this city. They're like the weather, like a thermometer: if it's warm, you see them around town, otherwise they are all in their rooms, holes, dorms, to study, fuck, and smoke. They're a carousel, an advertisement, like saying "Visit Perugia, the Middle Ages freshly conserved, little streets, alleyways, and heck, with the best international student body, an intellectual market: foreigners who stick their tongues, all their tongues, down the throat of the city and change its voice, its ideas, its vocal cords." Instead, it's nothing more than a cultural slogan.

They're all in a ghetto, separated from the people here. They float above them like oil in water, impossible to mix together. They come and go. The only thing they're good for is the prowl for a foreign girl or foreign boy, which always ends in never ending rejection.

Lina, the queen of fans, on a phone call on retreat in which Fabrizio and Bruno asked her if she swallowed or finished by jerking off when she did blowjobs, and gangbangs, and she replied yes, anything but taking it in the ass, that, not yet.

She called back, "I would like to see you nude, do you have a big ass? I am kind of homely, bottle shaped, one and sixty years old, grapple nosed. Would you like to make love? With all the women? Me, all day Sunday, up and down on the dick, ciao." Ciao.

Massage table, between the first half and the second, sweaty and sticky. Bubu making me uncomfortable working on my calves, suddenly it seems like the scene with the eye in that movie *Faccia di Spia*; the one where they were torturing that comrade, I don't know if in the Congo or in Angola. I can see the knife going in, digging into the blood, the eye in mush popping out. I feel like I can hear the sound, the same sound as when my uncle slaughtered a lamb, and he dug the knife right behind the eye too, turning it to make the hole bigger.

I remained horrified for several minutes, shivering. The calves, the massage, the match, the tiredness, the own goal by Niccolai, all vanished in that image of that bastard digging in the eye.

How it that possible, I wondered.

And I further wonder how it is that that sequence came rushing back over me. Certainly before I would let someone else cut me up I would do it to myself.

The latest from the Fascists. In the mail. An envelope: "To the comrade communist footballer Paolo Sollier, Avanguardia Operaia, Avanti! Social Center, Perugia Football Team." Inside is a copy of *Candido* with a photo of me glued under the title "You Will Be Buried in the Red Flag."

Amen.

To my consolation, there is a telegram: *Firmly condemning the Roman NeoFascist Riot against a person on the Perugia team we enthusiastically express our solidarity and admiration. Cordially, Lelmi, Francesco, President, ANPI San Giovanni Valdarno.*

Who knows if Gisella masturbates, and if so how. I thought of this one night while going to bed. I also tried to imagine her doing it, her legs large, her finger in the opening. But I wasn't able to. I have to ask her about it.

Anyway I declare officially over my love story with her, or rather, by myself. Ended by impotence, nothing else.

What I wanted I still want, and I'll smash the rest to pieces. There is only a change from vague hope to absolute certainty to not enter iton orbit, either around her or inside her.

But wouldn't you ever fall in love with me? she asks me in some field. "No!"

The right thing, the simplest, the shortest, the clearest. Said and amplified by all the repeaters in the brain, Swiss and Slovenes included. No and that's all. That's all.

Perugia-Juve 1-0, or how a little team can take the *scudetto* from the big team. The big team is comatose, mostly due to the performance of their players on the field. They argue among themselves, and the nicest thing they said to their manager Parola was up your ass.

What they said to us was fun too. One of them started it, telling us, "C'mon, we'll pay you more than Turin does, take it easy a little." And then there's the contemptuous, threatening type, Bettega. "If next year, you need a point, we'll give it to you, you can count on that...." As if in football there was ever anyone who helped you out. If they can crush you, they do, especially the big teams. In which case it is right to crush them, at least the few times it's possible to do so.

In any case, the nicest one is always Tardelli, who tells me, "C'mon, give me a penalty...." I honestly didn't know what face to make in reply.

The last exertion is in Switzerland, so that "Veronelli" can end his book with an international match. "Veronelli" is still Castagner. The nickname comes from the retreats. We're stuck in absurd hotels, gloomy and isolated from exhaustion, and he's going out Saturday night to dinner with the executives.

It's convenient to bring us to places like these, someone says, then he can leave. Shouldn't the manager share the fate of the team? So Zumbo invents "Veronelli." "Maybe he needs to write a gastronomy book, that's why he goes out. He has to take notes on the menu...."

In Switzerland, a match for our emigrants. When I read that a football match can represent revenge, satisfaction for the Italians living outside the country, I thought it was rhetoric. Revenge should be obtained by other means, I told myself. But I realized that it isn't always possible. That these comrades (they nearly all are) live being exploited, mistreated, ghettoized, without being able to react in any way. They are well-paid but they have to live badly, be seen with contempt, be mocked by the Swiss.

Winning the match was really satisfying, a kick in the ass to the Swiss. In the end we were super-tired, but happy; and there was no victory award. It was a friendly match to win a war.

These Swiss, clean to the point of being disgusting, are real stinkers. Spitting on their pavement is a duty, aside from a pleasure.

I am also pissed off. At the last campaign rally I had promised a leftist government and the collapse of the Christian Democrats. The results are that I have to go back to school, and learn the lesson a little better. My – our – forecasts for the demise of the Christian Democrats were overly optimistic. The DC shark ate the little fish, and remained very large. Of course, it now has less water to swim in. And it's a shark with strange teeth: white teeth, teeth that have been seized by the courts, teeth with cavities. Good as the dentist Zaccagnini is, they won't be able to all chew in unison. Better for everyone.

Proletarian Democracy should have done better. Some votes were siphoned off by Pannella, others by the PCI due to the alliance with Lotta Continua.

Anyway, it was a good lesson, above all because inside Lotta Continua big changes are bubbling. Also because the party constitution is something people are asking for, something in demand, something needed by the reality of the struggle. And we hope to have it soon.

The sporting slave trade exists: it's called the football transfer market. We, sold like fruit at a stand, who's buying, who's selling. We, without even a core like an apple, without will, without a way to intervene. I go to the Hotel Leonardo da Vinci with Walter and Patrizia, damned blondie. We mingle among the vendors, try to get a sense of the atmosphere. Walter gets a half hour of pats on the back and compliments, before anyone realizes he doesn't know anything. "What, they haven't told you?" What? says Walter. "You've been traded to Roma." Naturally he is happy, but the way he found out is terrible.

For me instead, the waters remain still. The deal with Rimini seems to have been ruined. "In all probability, you will stay in Perugia," they tell me. I even remember Castagner starting to make us do some jogging to arrive on retreat already warmed up.

Walter and I return to Perugia, discussing this shitty market, laughing about how he will be in Norcia, Rome and Perugia in the same place at the same time for training camp, how he will always be with us.

That evening, I go to sleep relaxed and I'm still on Perugia. When I wake up, I'm not anymore. I call headquarters to see if they reserved a place for me, and Sandrone answers. "Are you already in Rimini?" he asks me. What does Rimini have to do with anything I say, are you crazy? "But haven't you read the newspapers? You've been traded."

Ah. Very well. The right way to learn these things is to read it in the newspapers. Not a phone call, a whistle, a telegram from some executive Christ. You want us to treat fruits with respect?

Up your asses.

History lied,
Jesus Christ
was a midfielder.
Bought
with thirty dollars
-a lot for back then,
he had disappointed them a little.
He scored
very few miracles,
some of them were penalty shots anyway
and he was crucified by the press.
Judas in the end
invented the football transfer market.

I leave Perugia. I am really sorry; I said a lot of bad things about this city, but the way you do with someone you love, to get to know yourself better, so each of you is happier with the other. I have an almost sexual tension with her, she flows in my bloodstream, like I turned her upwind.

I'll be back.

I'm going to Rimini. A place for crazy people they say. Start another cartoon strip, "here's the noted footballer…."

NOTES

11
"commune": at times the situations that Sollier describes as communes are collective living conditions. The word "commune" was very common in the 1970s in Italy among social and political movements and the counterculture, as it was in the 1960s in the US. What seems to distinguish a commune from merely living with roommates in these pages is another element present in communes, partly ideological in nature, partly practical. The people involved have to have the goal of living differently, of an alternative social organization among themselves, based on different principles from the experience of finding roommates to share expenses based on chance encounters through the housing market. So "commune" has a political, one might almost say a spiritual aspect, beyond merely living together or doing something together.

"MIR" : the far left party in the Allende era Chile. "the Facchetti…": Giacinto Facchetti, Left Back for Milan in the 1970s.

13
Ilario Castagner was the manager of the Perugia team.

"Jacapone da Todi and the Wolves…": Jacapone da Todi, 1230-1306, was a Franciscan Friar who was a pioneer in developing theatre and dramatized gospel passages.

The Wolves of Gubbio are from a children's fairy tale story.

14
"retreat" – while in this passage Sollier is referring to the preseason training camp that is universal for teams around the world, Italian football teams have a unique practice of going on "retreat" – with players confined to their hotel or to the team's own training camp site for several days, usually as a way to address a losing streak, and may include actual training or practice, but may also instead be considered a chance to blow off steam, or to rest, reflect, and regroup.

"The Incredible Army...": *L'armata Brancaleone* – the movie with the title "For Love and Gold" in English, was a 1966 comedy.

15
"monument of Saint Benedict": In the main square in the town of Norcia, there is a statue of Saint Benedict where the Saint is portrayed with his hand open and several fingers pointed upward at angle that, in Sollier's reading at least, is somewhat suggestive.

"Marconcini": Roberto Marconcini, the Perugia goalkeeper.

19
Il Messaggero is a major daily newspaper based in Rome.
Nazione is a regional newspaper based in Florence.
Stadio is a sports newspaper, its title means "Stadium."

"all the herbs in one bundle": The word Sollier uses here is "fascio," which does mean "bundle" but is also a play on words that has obvious ideological implications.

"starved little bird": His dick, that is, since "uccello" – bird, is the usual slang term in Italian for a penis.

23
"Frate Mitra": The nickname, meaning "Friar Machinegun," of the Franciscan monk Silvano Girotto. Girotto had been in the French Foreign Legion, was a missionary in Bolivia, engaged in armed struggle in Chile and was a member of the Italian Red Brigades.

"open veins" – a reference to the classic work by Uruguayan writer Eduardo Galeano, *The Open Veins of Latin America*.

"the first '69 of my life": This refers to the mass wave of industrial strikes in the Italian "Hot Autumn" of 1969. Sollier had worked in FIAT factories before becoming a professional footballer.

24
"Pietro Valpreda" was an anarchist initially charged with the Piazza Fontana bombing of 1969, at a bank headquarters in Milan. He was declared "The monster of Piazza Fontana" by the Italian media, sat in prison for 15 years before his trial acquitted him on lack of evidence, and only 14 years after that was it discovered that a different person had committed the bombing.

25
"Sollier has to score, because the goalkeeper for the other team is named Borghese." – borghese is Italian for "bourgeois."

31
"Jonzac" is a town in southwestern France.

"Avanguardia Operaia": 'Workers Vanguard" – the party that Sollier was a member and activist in at the time.

35

"D'Attoma, Ghini": Franco D'Attoma was President of the Perugia Football Club, and Spartaco Ghini was Managing Director. Both were business owners, D'Attoma in clothing, Ghini in furniture and metalworking.

37

"Dutch retreat": This refers to the practice, associated in the 1970s with the Netherlands, of football teams bringing wives and girlfriends along during a team retreat in the 1970s.

40

"Lanfranco Ponziani": a well-known Italian sports journalist.
"*Quotidiano dei Lavoratori*": 'Workers Daily" – the party newspaper of Avanguardia Operaia.

Several footballers are referred to on this page, among whom:
"A Pruzzo to zero": Roberto Pruzzo, who played for Genoa 1973-1975.
Claudio Tenaglia, midfielder for Perugia, 1970-75.
Renato Curi midfielder for Perugia 1974-77.
Roberto Rosato, Defender for Genoa, 1973.1977.
Sergio Rossetti, Forward for Genoa, 1968-1977.
Pier Giuseppe Mosti, Defender, Genoa, 1973-1976.

41

"In an MSI office": Movimento Sociale Italiano – the Italian neofascist party after World War Two, it later changed its name to Allianza Nazionale.

43

"I go to the labor camps" – these are volunteer organizations that carry out socially useful activities.

44
"tempora mutand...": A play on a Latin phrase, that time changes all things, and on the Italian word for underwear, "mutande," which literally means a change (of underwear).

"*Quotidiano*": again refers to the *Quotidiano dei Lavoratori,* the Workers Daily newspaper of Avanguardia Operaia.

Servire il Popolo was the newspaper of the Maoist Italian (Marxist-Leninist) Communist Party.

"an old partisan": Someone who participated in the Italian Resistance against the Fascists and Nazis during the War.
"extras": throughout the book, Sollier refers to the extra-parliamentary left in Italy as the "extra-left," "extra-leftists" or "extras." The term "extra-parliamentary left" refers to all of the groups, organizations, thinkers, movements, protests, strikes, communes and other activities outside of the Italian Communist Party, the PCI, and usually far more militant and explicitly anti-capitalist than the Party and its activists and organizations.

46
"fight with Mariangela": Mariangela Sollier, Paolo's sister.

"Giani Mura": Mura's article gave Sollier his nickname as the "Compagno Centrovanti" – that is
"Comrade Centre-Forward." Mura was generally favorable to Sollier in his reporting, while those copying from Mura's reporting were not.

"article in 'Settimanale'": This refers to the newspaper *Il Settimanale del Movimento Sociale Italiana*, the weekly newspaper of the neofascist party the MSI.. The word "Settimanale" means "Weekly" in Italian.

Secolo d'Italia: As Sollier points out, another fascist newspaper of the time. The title means "The Century of Italy."

48

"Bentista" refers to Bente, the woman from Denmark that Sollier was involved with, the phrase of his invention, which he put on his doorbell, also rhymes with "Dentista" – that is, dentist.

Il Messaggero is a major daily newspaper based in Rome.

51

"I celebrate May Day and the 25th of April": May 1, May Day, is of course the International Workers Day. The 25th of April is Liberation Day in Italy, celebrating the fall of Fascism.
Silvano Ramaccioni was the sports director of the Perugia football club.

52

"centre-backward" a play on "centre-forward," Sollier's position on the field, and also an ideological dig at the backwardness of the politics of the fascist in question who was making threats on Sollier's life at the time.

54

Luigi Riva, Center-Forward for Cagliari 1963-76 and for the Italian National team, 1965-74, considered one of the greatest players of his time.

55

The poetry book title, *Chiodi e rose*, means "nails and roses."

Rina Dal Zilio, who authored several books of poetry while also continuing her career as a nurse in Treviso. Among her works of poetry are the collections *Briciole* (crumbs) 1976,

Le Ore della Sera (The evening hours) 1985, *Diario Evangelico* (Gospel diary) 1997, *e Cento Poesie d'amore* (one hundred love poems), 1996.

56
SPAL stand for Società Polisportiva Ars et Labor, a football club based in the city of Ferrara, in Serie B.

"Gente": The Italian word *gente* means "people" and Gente, an illustrated magazine, is entirely comparable to *People* magazine in the English-speaking world. *Paese Sera* is a national daily newspaper based in Rome.

Mauro Amenta was midfielder for Perugia for six Seasons.
Maurizio Marchei was a winger for Perugia from 1974-76.

Novella 2000 is a scandal and rumour-based tabloid newspaper focused on celebrities.

58
"*qualunquista*": Qualunquismo was a postwar phenomenon in Italy, based on the supposed ways of the "Uomo Qualunque," the "Anyman" or the Every Man, or the Common Man, eschewing politics and living a private life. Despite its "post-political" pretensions, it came to be seen as a precursor to later right wing political movements.

59
Quotidiano, again, is an abbreviation of the title of the newspaper *Quotidiano dei lavoratori*, "workers daily" of the organization *Avanguardia Operaia* which Sollier was a member of.

Il Manifesto is still a daily National leftist newspaper, unaffiliated with any organization or party, though it was founded by a left-wing faction within the PCI that was expelled from the Communist Party in 1969.

Lotta Continua was the daily newspaper of the extraparliamentary organization of the same name, which self-dissolved in 1978 after a famous national convention of the organization.

60
"UISP": The Unione Italiana Sport Popolare – now the Unione Italian Sport per Tutti is a sports association close historically to the Italian Communist and Socialist Parties.

61
Giancarlo "Zumbo" Raffaeli was a Defender for Perugia, 1973-76.

Foligno is a Serie D football club.

"lu centru de lu munnu" means "the center of the world" in dialect.

Walter Sabatini was Midfielder for Perugia 1973-75, and is now the Global Sporting Director for Bologna FC and for CF Montreal.

65
"MSI": Again, the postwar neofascist party, the Movimento Sociale Italiano.

"FUAN": Fronte Universitario d'Azione Nazionale – a neofascist student organization, founded in 1950 in Rome, and dissolved in 1996.

"a Constitution that prohibits…": Chapter XII of the Italian Constitution states, "E` vietata la riorganizzazione, sotto qualsiasi forma, del disciolto partito fascista.."
Translation: "Any reorganization, under any form, of the dissolved Fascist Party is prohibited."

66
"thirtieth anniversary": April 25, 1975, the 30th anniversary of the liberation of Italy from Fascism and from the Nazi Occupation of the country.

69
Giorgio Almirante, 1914-1988, was founder and leader of the neofascist party, the MSI.

70
"tanks in Prague": The 1968 Soviet invasion of Czechoslovakia, putting an end to the "Prague Spring."

The "Historic Compromise" was the name given to the policy of the PCI in the wake of the coup in Chile in 1973 against the Allende government, to seek an alliance with their traditional adversaries, the center-right Christian Democratic Party (DC). This in practice meant giving up any critical position toward government policy or toward social conditions, without getting much of anything in return. The extra-parliamentary left and the Autonomia movement of 1977 all strongly opposed the policy.

71
Paestum, near Naples, is the site of the largest ancient Greek ruins in Italy.

"his name is Miracolo": "Miracle" in Italian.

"training for the Nationals": for the Italian national team that is.

74

Giorgio Almirante was founder and leader of the MSI, the neofascist party in Italy.

Pietro Conti was the Communist mayor of Spoleto and member of parliament.

76

The Griffin: *Il Grifone,* is the nickname of the Genoa Football team.

Giorgio Molini: A legend of Perugia football, athletic trainer Giorgio Molini was known to the public as "il prof." – the professor.

Ilario Castagner was the manager of the Perugia team.

78

"Proletarian Democracy": Avanguardia Operaia participated in an electoral coalition with two other leftist groups, the Proletarian Unity Party (PdUP)) and the Workers Movement for Socialism (MLS) called Democrazia Proletaria in 1975. They obtained 1.5% of the vote. Three years later DP became a political party by the same name.

"even from the weather": "Tempo" means weather in Italian, as well as time. So the name of the publication "Tempo" that Sollier refers to allows him to make a play on words regarding the weather and not the publication by that name, becoming another thing Proletarian Democracy had to defend itself against.

79
"Demofanfani": Fanfani was at the time leader of the Christian Democratic Party, known as the Democristiani.

The Curva is the part of the stadium behind each goal and is where the team's most fervent supporters stand during the match. In the typical architecture of Italian football stadiums, it curves, making the overall football stadium ovular in shape. I have chosen to not translate it as "curve" since the concept of the Curva is unique to Italian football, and has the cultural and sociological meaning that Sollier attributes to it.

The fans at the Curva are often the Ultras, the most dedicated and often fanatical (the etymological origin of the word "fan"), and in many locales are also associated with the far-right politically. This is certainly true of Lazio, one of the two teams of Serie A based in Rome for example (the other "Roma" tends to be associated with the political left). For more on the Ultras, see Tobias Jones, *Ultra: The Underworld of Italian Football* (2021: Head of Zeus).

"holiday boxes": In Italian stadiums, the "tribuna" is where the VIPs, wealthy fans, and other dignitaries sit, secluded from the other parts of the stadium. The tribuna is the social equivalent, therefore, of reserved box seats in American sports stadiums, or the hospitality boxes along the side of a pitch in British football.

82
"Larzac": From 1971 to 1981, farmers on the Larzac plateau in south-western France engaged in mass nonviolent civil disobedience to oppose extension of a military base. The farmers won when newly elected President Francois Mitterand cancelled the planned extension.

84
Tuttosport is a national sports newspaper.

"The Nationals": the Nationals were a popular brands of cigarettes at the time.

88
Giorgio Chinaglia, a striker for Lazio from 1969-76, who had previously played for Swansea Town (1964-66), and who, in 1976, went to the US to play for the New York Cosmos professional football (soccer) team.

92
"CGIL-CISL-UIL": The umbrella coalition of the three largest trade union federations in Italy, the traditionally left-wing (formerly PCI-affiliated) Confederazione Generale Italiana del Lavoro, the historically Christian Confederazione Italiana Sindacati Lavoratori, and the historically moderate socialist Unione Italiana del Lavoro.

93
Giuseppe Wilson was a footballer born in northern England, played centre-back for Internapoli, 1965-69, Lazio 1969-80, and on loan from Lazio for the New York Cosmos. He also played for the Italian national team.

Sergio Petrelli, defender who played from 1964-1982 for Carrera, Verona, Roma and Lazio, among other teams. While playing for Lazio, he fired pistol shots to scare away Roma fans that had come to the hotel where Lazio players were staying to jeer the team at night.

Sergio Campana was a striker to Vicenza and Bologna in the 1960s, then President of the Associazione Italian di Calciatori, the Footballers Association, from 1968 to 2011.

Claudio Pasqualin was a lawyer, and became the General Secretary of the Footballers Association in 1972, and served as Vice-president for nearly a decade.

94
"Doit": "Facete" is grammatically incorrect, since the second person plural of " to do" – fare – is "fate." I have translated this word as "doit" instead of "get" or "make it happen" to capture the sense of dissonance that Sollier intends here.

D'Attoma says "Voaltri" – dialect for a plural "you." It literally would mean "you others" and is a popular form of expression in parts of northern Italy, but is not Italian. I have translated it with the US South's equally colloquial but grammatically incorrect plural of "you" in English, "you all."

95
For Carlos Monzòn, the Argentine boxer and one-time undisputed Middleweight Champion of the world, who was well-known in Italy for his two fights (and victories) against Italian Nino Benvenuti, in 1970 and 1971.

97
Gino Bartali won the Tour de France in 1948, which ran from 30 June to 25 July; Palmiro Togliatti, General Secretary of the Italian Communist Party was shot by a Fascist student on 14 July. Togliatti survived the assassination attempt.

99
"campanilistic": In Italian, "campanilismo" refers to the widespread loyalty to the local neighborhood or village or town, as symbolized by the local parish bell-tower, the "campana." It is used in contrast to wider loyalties to nation, party, class or universal values. But it is not identified as an ethnic, racial or even party-ideological adherence. Merely "parochialism."

Filbert Bayi Sanka, of Tanzania, set the world records for running 1500 metres in 1974, and 1975.

101
Luciano Re Cecconi, was a Midfielder for Lazio, 1972-77, and for the Italian National team in 1974, and known for his sense of humor. He was shot to death in 1977 while pretending to rob a friend's jewelry store in Rome as a practical joke.

Novellinosettantasei: A clever play on words by Sollier's adversary journalist here, since the player's name "Novellino" is similar to "Novella" in the title of the scandal sheet that Sollier had linked that journalist to with his own nickname for D'Orsi noted earlier. The nickname he gives in reply to Sollier uses the name of the player that has replaced him as a regular, Novellino, and is itself a play on words that could be translated, "the little scandal of '76."

102
Pier Paolo Pasolini, the writer and film maker. Pasolini was murdered on 2 November, 1975, by being run over several times by his own car, after being brutally beaten.

109
"Mogadon": The brand name of Nitrezepan, a hypnotic drug used for short-term relief from severe anxiety and insomnia.

"a day of vacation": Here, Sollier uses another clever play on words: "Vacanza" is vacation in Italian, vacca is a somewhat insulting word for "cow" and "boia" meaning executioner, is often used in phrases to form curse words. In this case, "vacca boia" which is untranslatable in literary terms (executioner cow), but he adds a second "c" to vacanza to render the phrase "un giorno di vacca boia (which I have translated as "doing fuck all," a day of "vaccanza").

112
Enrico Berlinguer was General Secretary of the Communist Party from 1972-1984.

"the historic bullshit": refers to the Historic Compromise between the PCI and the Christian Democrats.

The "curva": again, a reference to the curved parts of the stands in Italian stadiums, which are an important part of the culture of the so-called "ultras" or the most intense fans of the team, seated behind the goals.

114
L'Unità was the one-time and long-time newspaper of the Communist Party.

"Chiaraguism": This refers to the practice of falling to the ground faking an injury, attributed to the Forward for AC Milan and Napoli in the 1970s, Luciano Chiarugi, leading the Italian press to create the term "chiarugismo" to label the practice.

116
Flipper was a television dolphin.

"Outstretched Hands": "Mani Tese" is an Italian NGO founded in 1964 that engages in charity service work to poor communities around the world.

118
"Casadei Orchestra": A famous dance music orchestra in Italy, seriously kitsch in self-presentation.

121

Giuseppina Manin wrote on Culture for many years in *Corriere della Sera*, the leading newspaper in Italy. She also worked on four books together with Dario Fo, the Nobel Prize for literature winner, long associated with the extraparliamentary left.

"Montanellian": Indro Montanelli was a conservative journalist and historian of Italy, dead in 2001, but who recently became infamous for his fascist youth, and for having bought and married a 12-year old Eritrean girl, an issue that became a subject of Black Lives Matter protests internationally.

123

"rabbleman": The word for "rabble" or "mob" in Italian is Marmaglia – a feminine noun. Gisella's invented word is "Marmaglio" – creating a masculine form of the word for effect.

124

"a Lanzi": Enrico Lanzi, defender for Perugia, who also played for Milan. A big, physically impressive man, popular with women, he was viewed with some jealousy by the other players for his handsome, rugged looks and attractiveness.

Breda refers to an important metal-working company founded in Milan.

125

Mario Tanassi, a leader of the Social Democratic Party the PSDI, a party allied with the Christian Democrats, and founded as part of CIA efforts to split the Socialist Party and divide the left, was charged by the Italian Constitutional Court of involvement in the Lockheed Bribery scandal. He was found guilty in 1979 and spent four months in prison.

Renato Zaccarelli was a midfielder for several teams in the 1970s.

Benigno Zaccagnini, a Christian Democratic politician, and follower of Aldo Moro, who later, while a prisoner of the Red Brigades who later murdered him, accused his protégé Zaccagnini of sacrificing him in order to save the new government of which he was a minister.

Giulio Andreotti was the most powerful politician in Italy for decades, a leader of the Christian Democrats, and a symbol for leftists of everything wrong with the more than five decades-long reign of that party in power. He was also hunchbacked, and relatively short.

"choose a lion": Both Andreotti and Luìs Vinìcio, born Luis Vinicius de Menezes in Brazil, were known as "the lion" or Neapolitan dialect "o lione" in their respective fields. Vinicio, as he was known, played his whole career as a center forward in Italy, including for Naples from 1955-1960. He later managed the Naples team in the 1970s, during the period in which Sollier is writing.

127
"from Meucci": Antonio Meucci was an Italian inventor and associate of Giuseppe Garibaldi, credited with inventing a voice-communication device that many see as the first working telephone. Italians credit Meucci, not Alexander Graham Bell, with the invention of the modern telephone.

Ras le bol : French for "fed up."

129

"Sollier boia" was the Italian phrase used by the Lazio fans/fascists. "Boia," technically meaning "executioner" in Italian, is used colloquially, including in politics by both the far right and far left, as a generic term of insult, and is not usually an actual reference to the person as a killer, let alone a state executioner. So I have rendered it "asshole," which is its functional use at least in American English. The British equivalent might be rendered as "cunt."

132

"five or six thousand liras": about 2-3 Euros, 2 British pounds, or 3 US dollars, not adjusted for inflation.

In the old lira system, 500 million lire were worth about $200,000 to $250,000 US, depending on variations in the exchange rate over time.

"Reserve Clause": the "Vincolo sportivo" – an institution in Italian sports that prevents players from leaving teams, and requires an indemnity paid to the original team should a player move on. The situation in Italy for professional football was therefore similar to that in most of Europe before the EU Court's Bosman ruling.

In 1981, the *vincolo sportivo* for professional sports was done away with, and players are now only obligated to remain with teams for the duration of the contract, which cannot exceed 5 years at a time. It is still in legal force for amateur sports, and levels below the professional. I have translated it using the analogous rule that governed American baseball very famously (or infamously) the reserve clause, that prevented players from changing teams at their will, even at the end of a contract.

The meniscus is the part of the knee that is most frequently injured in football.

135
The "Festa dell'Unità" is an annual gathering and celebration organized by and to raise funds for L'Unità, then the PCI, now ex-Communist Party newspaper, which takes the form of concerts, barbecues, speakers, events and something of a county fair in all the large and medium-size cities of Italy.

Sister Pagliuca was a nun arrested in 1969 for mistreatment of children who were in the care of the Istituto Santa Rita in the town of Gottaferrata.

136
"divo" would be the masculine form of the Italian word, by now international, "diva."

142
Faccia di Spia, also released in English as *C.I.A. The Secret Story*, is a leftwing 1975 Italian film by Giiuseppe Ferrara, about the CIA's misdeeds during the 1950s, 60s and 70s, told through recreations.

Candido was a pro-monarchist satirical weekly magazine that ceased publication in 1961.

143
ANPI, *Associazione Nazionale Partigiani d'Italia*, is the National Association of Italian Partisans, the veterans of the Italian Antifascist Resistance, the telegram to Sollier coming from their chapter in the town of San Giovanni Valdarno, in Tuscany.

145
"Juve": Juventus.

"scudetto": The scudetto is a small shield-shaped symbol sown into the uniforms of, and worn by the championship-winning team in Italian football.

Luigi Veronelli was a restaurant and wine critic.

147
"Pannella": Marco Pannella, founder and leader of the civil liberties-oriented Radical Party.

"inside Lotta Continua big changes are bubbling." Sollier was quite right. At its National convention that November, 1976, Lotta Continua dissolved itself after tense ideological conflicts

FURTHER READING

ON FOOTBALL AND RADICAL POLITICS
Gabriel Kuhn, *Soccer vs. the State: Tackling Football and Radical Politics* (2011, PM Press)
Will Simpson and Malcolm McMahon, *Freedom Through Football: The Story of the Easton Cowboys and Cowgirls: Inside Britain's Most Intrepid Sports Club* (2012, Tangent Books)
Carles Viñas and Natxo Parra, *St. Pauli: Another Football is Possible* (2020, Pluto Books)

ON ITALIAN FOOTBALL
John Foot, *Calcio: A History of Italian Football* (2007: Harper)
John Foot, *Winning at All Costs: A Scandalous History of Italian Soccer* (2007: Nation Books)
Tobias Jones, *Ultra: the Underworld of Italian Football* (2021: Head of Zeus)
Gianluca Vialli, *The Italian Job: A Journey to the Heart of Two Great Footballing Cultures* (2007: Bantam)

ON THE EXTRA-PARLIAMENTARY LEFT AND MOVEMENTS IN ITALY IN THE 1970S
Patrick Gun Cunningham, *Autonomia: A Movement of Refusal: Social Movements and Social Conflicts in Italy in the 1970s* (2002), Middlesex University, available at: https://eprints.mdx.ac.uk/6688/
Robert Lumley, *States of emergency: cultures of revolt in Italy from 1968 to 1978* (1990, Verso)
Toni Negri, *Books for Burning: Between Civil War and Democracy in 1970s Italy* (2005: Verso)
Steve Wright, *Storming Heaven: Class Composition and Struggle in Italian Autonomist Marxism* (2017: Pluto).

ON PERUGIA
Keith Kollman, *Italy – La Dolce Vita: Living in Perugia in the 1970s* (2020) (available only in Kindle edition)

ON THE COMMUNIST PARTY AND THE HISTORIC COMPROMISE
Ioannis Balampanidis, *EuroCommunism: From the Communists to the Radical European Left* (2018: Routledge)

FOR GENERAL HISTORY OF ITALIAN POLITICS AND CULTURE SINCE WORLD WAR II
Patrick McCarthy, *Italy Since 1945* (2000: Oxford University Press)